Zest for Life

Hay House Titles of Related Interest

BOOKS

An Attitude of Gratitude, by Keith D. Harrell
Discover Yourself, by Lillian Too
Gratitude: A Way of Life, by Louise L. Hay
Inner Peace for Busy People, by Joan Z. Borysenko, Ph.D.
Life Is Short—Wear Your Party Pants, by Loretta LaRoche
Life's a Journey–Not a Sprint, by Jennifer Lewis-Hall
Longevity in Action, by Arnold Bull
Soul Coaching, by Denise Linn

CARD DECKS

Empowerment Cards, by Tavis Smiley
I Can Do It® Cards, by Louise L. Hay
Inner Peace Cards, by Dr. Wayne W. Dyer
The 7 Habits of Highly Effective People®, by Stephen R. Covey
Tips for Daily Living, by Iyanla Vanzant

All of the above are available at your local bookstore, or may be ordered by visiting:
Hay House USA: **www.hayhouse.com**
Hay House Australia: **www.hayhouse.com.au**
Hay House UK: **www.hayhouse.co.uk**
Hay House South Africa: **orders@psdprom.co.za**

Zest for Life

Dawn Breslin

HAY HOUSE, INC.
Carlsbad, California
London • Sydney • Johannesburg
Vancouver • Hong Kong

Published and distributed in the United States by: Hay House, Inc., P.O. Box 5100, Carlsbad, CA 92018-5100 • *Phone:* (760) 431-7695 or (800) 654-5126 • *Fax:* (760) 431-6948 or (800) 650-5115 • www.hayhouse.com • **Published and distributed in Australia by:** Hay House Australia Pty. Ltd., 18/36 Ralph St., Alexandria NSW 2015 • *Phone:* 612-9669-4299 • *Fax:* 612-9669-4144 • www.hayhouse.com.au • **Published and distributed in the United Kingdom by:** Hay House UK, Ltd. • Unit 62, Canalot Studios • 222 Kensal Rd., London W10 5BN • *Phone:* 44-20-8962-1230 • *Fax:* 44-20-8962-1239 • www.hayhouse.co.uk • **Published and distributed in the Republic of South Africa by:** Hay House SA (Pty), Ltd., P.O. Box 990, Witkoppen 2068 • *Phone/Fax:* 2711-7012233 • orders@psdprom.co.za • **Distributed in Canada by:** Raincoast • 9050 Shaughnessy St., Vancouver, B.C. V6P 6E5 • *Phone:* (604) 323-7100 • *Fax:* (604) 323-2600

Design: Jim Banting, e-Digital

Library of Congress Cataloging-in-Publication Data

Breslin, Dawn
 Zest for life : 10 dynamic life-changing solutions for self-empowerment / Dawn Breslin.
     p. cm.
  ISBN 1-4019-0331-2 (pbk.)
  1. Self-actualization (Psychology) 2. Self-perception. I. Title.
  BF637.S4B735 2004
  158.1—dc22

                          2003026425

                 ISBN 1-4019-0331-2

        07 06 05 04   4 3 2 1
            1st printing, April 2004

        Printed in the United States of America

For Liberty
with so much
LOVE XX

CONTENTS

Dawn's Story   xi
The 10 Golden Rules   xix
Introduction   xxv

PART I: GETTING SOME ZEST IN YOUR LIFE

One: How Our Thoughts Create Our World   1
Two: As Children We Are Perfect   7
Three: The Stepping-Stones on Our Life Journey   21
Four: What's Shaping Your Life?   29
Five: Understanding the Power of the Mind   35
Six: How Would You Love Your Life to Be?   53
Seven: The Power of Positive Affirmations   63
Eight: The Five Magical Ingredients   79
Nine: The Mind-Body Connection   99
Ten: Making Every Day Special   109
Eleven: The Big Stuff   127

PART II: DEALING WITH THE TOUGH STUFF—
             HEALING A BRUISED SOUL

Twelve: Creating Some Powerful Foundations   147
Thirteen: Learning to Love Ourselves Again   157
Fourteen: Clearing the Pain of the Past   169
Fifteen: Living for Today   183
Sixteen: Connecting with the World   191

Dawn's Story . . . As This Book Comes to an End   205

"Dawn Breslin is one of the top teachers around today. She has an enormous zest for life, which she shares with great enthusiasm. Dawn can take you from despair to the top of the world—and can totally change your life for the better while she's doing it."

— Louise L. Hay,
the best-selling author of
You Can Heal Your Life

Dawn's Story

Before I was a mom, I worked in the field of
advertising, and I was one of the highest achievers
in the UK. I'd produced exceptional results and was
earning around $90,000 by the time I was 22 years
old. I'd traveled a large chunk of the world on my own
by the time I was 24. To the outside world I had it all—
a beautiful home, a husband who loved me, a wonderful social
life, and lots of money. And here I was, at the age of 26, about
to embark upon the greatest challenge of my life so far!

When I gave birth to Liberty, she was the most gorgeous little being with beautiful big brown eyes. Within seconds of being born, she was clamped to my breast, feeding like she had known me all her life—which of course she had! Liberty's dad and I were so proud, and life felt like a daydream. I was so happy.

When Liberty was three weeks old, she developed colic and the crying didn't stop for seven months.

I thought that being a mother would be the most natural and easy thing I'd ever have to do in my life. For me it couldn't have been further from the truth—in reality, for the first six months of my daughter's life, motherhood was the most difficult thing I had ever done, and I felt like I was failing . . . fast. I had never really failed before. What a shock to my system! As a new mother, all you want is for your child to be content, and to feel pride in the way you are helping nurture and grow your little being. I remember when people said to me, "Isn't she just beautiful?" I would smile, but inside I said. *Yes—but she just cries constantly and I can't cope. You have no idea what I'm going through; I am so exhausted.*

I was struggling with everything in my life—my baby, my relationship, and my social life. I had put on weight and felt unhappy with the way I looked. Once I had been in control, and now it felt as if life had closed in on me. I felt like a mouse caught in a trap, stuck inside my own inner world, and I was frightened to tell anyone. I was convinced that people would remind me of how hundreds of women give birth to children and raise whole families on their own while their husbands are at work, and they cope. I had my husband as well as my mother around, and I only had one child, so what was my problem?

The more difficult I found it to cope with my daughter crying from morning until night, the more upset I became, and the more upset Liberty was becoming. After six months of feeling useless and exhausted, my self-esteem and confidence were dropping to an all-time low.

These were the most frightening feelings I had experienced in my entire life. Traveling alone in Cambodia held no comparison!

In my mind, each day felt black, and the doors to the future seemed firmly closed. I had real difficulty imagining my life beyond each day. I painted on a face to present to the outside world, but inside I was so unhappy.

I didn't want to talk to my family, my nurse, my doctor, or friends, as I felt that would have meant admitting failure. I was terrified. I thought that this feeling would last forever; and when you find yourself in this place, you don't know what's happening to you. Each day I felt trapped and very alone. I was living in a world where I felt I had no choices and there was no light at the end of the tunnel. I had no history of depression, and therefore didn't know how to go about getting better.

At that point in my life, I had no idea that I was suffering from post-partum depression. Then, luckily, someone told me that I could feel much better and that I could vastly improve my life if I were to change the way I thought about myself and change some of my everyday habits. I thought this was the biggest load of rubbish I'd ever heard. However, I had two choices: I could opt for Prozac or I could try to make some changes. Here I am, seven years later, enthusiastically writing a book about my amazing life journey. I now have a burning passion to share what I've learned with people who really would like to turn their lives around and get so much MORE.

It seemed like a twist of fate when my dear Aunt Margaret guided me to a two-day *You Can Heal Your Life* workshop developed by inspirational teacher Louise L. Hay. At the workshop, I realized that I actually had a lot of options open to me in my life—if only I could begin to change the way I thought about myself as "me" and as a mother. I realized that as long as I lived my life authentically and in alignment with my core belief system rather than how I thought my life should be, then everyone would benefit.

One of my many fundamental realizations was that I really wanted to go back to work. Working life was how I could exercise my creativity, and my core belief was that moms should be able to work either full- or part-time and look after a family. My own mother had done that, and I couldn't see any challenges in it; but somehow I had also inherited a belief along the lines of "Good moms stay at home, and if you don't do that, as a mother you will be a failure."

When we made a list of all the things that we believed we should do in our lives, I wrote that I should be at home with my child full-time. At that moment I saw how what I had written wasn't in alignment with my authentic feelings. If we don't do things that we feel on a deep level are right for us, we begin to live out of our truth and allow uneasiness or dis-ease into our lives. I realized that I had lost respect for myself; I loathed who I had become. I thought I was unattractive and use-less. My self-esteem was so low that I questioned whether I was ever going to succeed if

I went back to work again. Over these two days, I began to put my life back into some perspective. Just because I hadn't utilized any of my talents or qualities for a while didn't mean that they had gone away forever. I had just temporarily lost sight of how capable and able I really was.

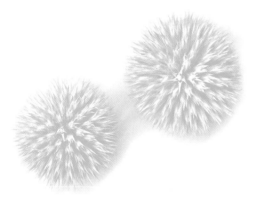

It was hugely liberating to confront all of this. What I learned at the workshop was common sense. I learned about understanding the way we think, and how what we think every day impacts the way we feel; ultimately our thoughts are responsible for shaping our lives. This was a revelation to me. Thinking back to when I had been successful, I had a strong, encouraging dialogue running in my head every day, and people would remark on how upbeat, positive, and enthusiastic I was about life. I saw how, just at the time when I began to have feelings of uselessness and failure, the way I thought about myself changed fundamentally. I began to assess my success in life based on my experience of becoming a mother—the one thing that hadn't worked out the way I'd imagined. I had replaced my positive, upbeat inner dialogue with one that was making me feel low.

When this happens, it's almost as if we go into a downward spiral, and over the period of a year my dialogue had completely changed. As a result, my self-confidence and my self-esteem began to deteriorate. Before I had postpartum depression, I didn't really know what self-confidence and self-esteem were. I guess when you have an abundance of it, you don't need to know; however, when it's lacking, you know something is wrong, and although you don't know what it is, the search begins to find out how you can get it back! That's if you have the energy.

As I write this, I'm reflecting back to the time when I felt numb, and how it was a twist

"...what we think every day impacts on the way we feel; ultimately our thoughts are responsible for shaping our lives."

of fate that I managed to go to the workshop. I was opening up to no one, there was no advice available, and short of going to the doctor for medication, I wouldn't have known where to look for help. I found the richest solution around, self-empowering help that made me even stronger than when I first started out. If I hadn't, who knows where I would be today? In my case I didn't have a clue what was lacking, but the feelings were very unpleasant.

• I worried about all the little things.
• I never did anything "just for me," as I felt I wasn't deserving.
• I was stressed out and yet I never took any time out to relieve the stress.
   • I was insecure and fearful about my personal life.
      • I was insecure about my future and about getting a job again.
      • I thought I wasn't interesting and I didn't deserve love and attention.
• I felt I was a lousy mother although I spent every waking hour with my child.
• I was eating for comfort and was dissatisfied with my body and face.
• I felt judgmental and critical of myself and others.
• I had low tolerance and would feel frustrated.

I can remember watching talk shows on TV and crying, empathizing with people's pain, and how the program with UK presenter Lorraine Kelly became my glamorous daily highlight. My brain felt like it had shut down. Some days living in this vacuum was okay; on other days it felt frightening. Looking back, it's interesting that initially, the feelings were of lack and failure about being a mother; however, they gradually spread into everything I was doing until I eventually questioned my relationship, my social skills, my ability to go for an interview, how I looked, how interesting I was . . . it got so bad I thought I'd be better off on my own rather than endure the pain of being with others. The constant barrage of negative thinking every day was forming my self-perceptions, and in turn, these beliefs were holding me back from any real joy in my life.

SOMETHING HAD TO CHANGE!

At the workshop I was so excited and over-joyed when I realized this, and for the first time in almost 12 months, I could see a way forward. It was a fantastic feeling. I could almost feel the world and all the possibilities of life open up again.

I compared the sort of life that I thought I should be living and the sort of life that I really wanted to live. The gap was huge . . . and that's where the hard work began.

"I could almost feel the world and all the possibilities of life open up again."

Gradually I began to repair and replace the dialogue I had developed at the point when I had lost my focus and direction, and about three months later I began to bounce back to my confident self again. It wasn't a straightforward process—it took time and hard work as I had to change so many of the habits that I'd developed, and that's a tough process to begin. I had to learn to put myself first more often, I had to learn to create time for me to replenish my energy, I had to relax and nurture my bruised soul, and I had to de-stress to release the creativity that I thought I'd lost.

At the workshop I had caught sight of the real me, and at times I was in tears as I was faced with being really honest with myself about my life. This process was pretty painful, but I realized that to make a really new start in my life and to be true to myself, there were some key issues I had to deal with. I felt that if I did not begin to act now, the feelings of being stuck would never lift. I had to make some fundamental life changes, which sadly involved reviewing my marriage. My husband and I separated six months later. This was the right thing to do.

I realized at the workshop that there were hundreds, if not thousands, of people just like me. It was a great feeling to realize that in this place, I was not alone. When the workshop ended, we were all invited to choose a card with a single word on it to give us encouragement for the future. My word was PURPOSE! That was the beginning of my journey. On the day I drew the card out of the bag, I remember vividly thinking that it was now my job to take what I had learned out to the world. I had a passion to communicate the message that even when it feels like the world is tumbling down on top of you and there are no choices left, you really can make changes if you are prepared to put in the hard work.

I wanted to take this material out in a very public fashion: This was my purpose! I dreamed of giving seminars, I wanted to get into TV and media, and I wanted newspapers and magazines to publish stories about it; however, my biggest challenge was that I was absolutely terrified of speaking in public. I had never done it before, and it scared the living daylights out of me. I was petrified of going on TV, and the first time a journalist pressed the record button on his tape recorder for me to give my opinion on a workshop that I attended, my mouth dried up! I had so many ambitions, but so many fears to overcome. I now regularly appear on TV in the UK and overseas, I am an advisor on the board of *Here's Health* magazine, and national magazines and newspapers are constantly interviewing me. I have my own TV series on Discovery Health, my books will reach readers all over the world, and my ambition is to touch the millions of people who really need this kind of encouragement but have never had it before.

If this sounds like you, then you are just like I was not so long ago. Since my workshop seven years ago, I have been on a very exciting journey of self-discovery. If you can relate to any part of my story, this book is my gift to you. Here, I will talk about the techniques that I learned

"I had so many ambitions and fears."

to help me overcome my fears, I'll discuss the formulas that I used to achieve my goals, and on the whole I'll share ALL of my success secrets with you so that you can take them, try them, and test them. I really believe that by boosting our confidence and self-esteem, we have the key to creating authentic joy in our lives. I've conquered fears, achieved goals, and changed my perception of myself and people around me. I live life to the fullest and no challenge is too great. Having said that, it's been tough, and there have been moments when I have fallen down, but with what I have learned in the last seven years, I now have a whole range of coping strategies to pick myself back up, dust myself off, and get on with it all over again!

When your life feels like it's caving in, or when you just can't seem to achieve something that is your dream, this book will help guide you toward some real-life solutions and strategies to help move you forward.

Please read it from cover to cover, because the one thing that could be your biggest issue or block could be the very thing that is in one of the chapters that you miss out on. My passion in writing this book has grown hugely over the last few years. The more I have learned, the more I feel a great need to share this information with as many people as I can. I truly believe that this stuff should be taught in schools to prepare us for the inevitable challenges that we face in this game of life!

I hope that this book can become a type of self-help bible for you. My goal is to meet you at the point where you are right now in your life, using tried and tested formulas that can help you lift the quality of your life to a higher level. I'll share my own life experiences and the experience that I have gathered from hundreds of people who have gone through my *Zest for Life* workshops. As you work your way through the book, I'll take you through some very thought-provoking exercises. I'll ask you to question your life, inside out and upside down. I'll then share with you some ideas and methods to gently help you begin to introduce some powerful coping strategies into your life.

Part I answers these questions:

• Who are you really?
• What shaped you?
• What do you have to change to make life a joy?
• Why do you feel the way you do?
• What do you really want from life?
• What stops you from getting it?

In Part II, we begin to deal with the Tough Stuff, powerful material that helps you build a real foundation for your life, deal with your internal and external dialogue and interactions, and build your self-esteem and self-confidence to make you feel so much better about yourself. This includes:

• boosting self-confidence;
• boosting self-esteem;
• letting go of pain;
• removing guilt; and
• overcoming shyness.

Using this book can help you design a more authentic, calm, and peaceful style of living; achieve the success you've always wanted; or reach the dizzy heights of lifetime ambitions—you mold it to your needs. Whatever you want from the book, there are just 10 Golden Rules to keep in mind as you work your way through . . .

The 10 Golden Rules

This book is about you—it's about realizing what
your qualities are and reminding yourself of them daily.
It's about recognizing that you deserve to be loved and
respected by people around you, and understanding that
you need to respect yourself to get the best out of life and
feel good each day. So often we live our lives doing what
everyone else wants us to do, and by diverting our attention to other people's needs and interests, we are never
truly aware of our own.

By following these 10 Golden Rules, we are going to work through this book and make you aware of what you truly deserve in your life—and then show you how to get it! Right now this may feel a little alien, but if you work your way through, do the necessary exercises, and follow the techniques, you will begin to feel completely different.

RULE 1

Be patient with yourself. Please give this book a try, even if you aren't someone who usually reads self-help books. You'll find it full of exciting exercises to learn more about yourself and move you forward in your life. Try reading just one page at a time.

RULE 2

You deserve this chance to make some positive changes in your life, even if you do feel that life is too heavy or it would be selfish of you to make changes. Please take this opportunity to explore the possibilities. What have you got to lose? Nothing ventured, nothing gained. This could be the best thing you have ever done.

RULE 3

Treat yourself . . . make this your daily or bedtime ritual. Find at least ten minutes a day to read it, even if it's in the bathroom! If you can do a chapter a day, take the time and try not to read it any faster, as you will need time to digest the exercises and really think about the material. How often have you picked up books, read the theory, and never implemented the techniques?

RULE 4

Be gentle with yourself . . . nobody is perfect and we can all make mistakes—we are human, after all! To date you have only done the best you could with the knowledge that you had at the time. Try not to be harsh with yourself about the way you have lived your life—there is no rule book we all have to follow. You have done your best and that's okay—today is your new window for change. The choice is yours.

RULE 5

The past is in the past . . . this book is about *now*. Today you have a chance to make a difference in your life. No amount of guilt about yesterday is of any value to you. Focus on the future as we move through the chapters. (I know it's easier said than done, but please just make an effort to give it a try. There's a whole section on letting go in here.)

RULE 6

Be honest with yourself . . . so often we avoid the truth to avoid change. If something in this book touches a nerve, or if you feel a pain in your tummy or in your chest, this is a sign that something isn't sitting easily with you. Listen to what you are feeling at this point and if you can, write it down in a journal. Pretending only keeps you stuck in pain.

RULE 7

Record your feelings. Buy a journal or scrapbook and write down what you think and feel as you move through the exercises. Make it a special book that you like the look and feel of. Keep it by your side or in a private place as you work through this guidebook.

RULE 8

Share what you find with people who will support and encourage you. Don't ever share your feelings or ambitions with people who will challenge you or put you down. This will take you back to square one. When we are encouraged and supported, change can take rapid effect.

RULE 9

Find a photo of yourself as a five-year-old child. If you don't have a photo, ask anyone who might have one to give it to you. If you can, have it blown up and framed. This is important if you want to get the best from this book, because you will need the photo often as we work through the exercises. You can also use the photo as a bookmark.

RULE 10

Trust. We are born with instincts, so listen to your inner voice as you work through these exercises. When we clear away the debris, we can hear what we really need to hear. Listen up for that voice in your head as you journey through this book. Record your thoughts and feelings in your journal. Just explore to begin with—you won't ever need to do anything that you don't want to. Please just have the courage to record how you really feel. One day, if you want to or if you find the courage, you could make the changes . . . but only if you choose.

"When we are encouraged and supported, change can take rapid effect."

Zest for Life Workshops

Before we start, I want to give you a taste of what you can expect if you make the choice to put all this into practice in your life. I have been running workshops for five years now, and have worked with people on a whole range of things they wanted to deal with, including the following:

- Being laid off
- Wanting to go back to work but not having the confidence
- Being bullied
- Feeling depressed
- Wanting to leave a marriage
- Wanting to spend more time with the kids
- Losing a business
- Wanting to save a marriage
- Wanting to improve sales figures
- Wanting to set up a company/business

- Hating yourself and not knowing what's wrong
- Wanting a relationship
- Being in abusive relationships
- Needing to rebuild life after being widowed
- Being single and unable to meet anyone
- Struggling to lose weight
- Getting a balance in life

I have files that bulge from all the thank-you letters I've received. Here are a couple of brief case studies of two capable human beings who temporarily lost sight of their potential. As you read through this book, you'll find lots of similar stories.

Getting Laid Off

Bill was in a very successful position at a large bank. He was 45 years old and had been with the bank since he was 21. He had worked his way up and loved his job. Bill was very confident about his abilities in marketing, and with his knowledge and expertise, he really made a mark in his department. He had always felt secure in his life.

One morning Bill was called into his boss's office, where a company announcement was about to be made to the whole team. Due to reorganization, Bill was being laid off. Over the following weeks, Bill's confidence began to drop. He considered applying for a new job, but he began to doubt himself; he thought he was too old for the job market, and too set in his ways to join another company.

Over the next month or so, he become withdrawn from his wife and she began to feel the impact of his situation, too. A month later, when Bill's interviews weren't going too well, Bill began to feel increasingly out of sorts and went to the doctor, who said that she thought stress had upset his system. She offered him some light medication.

A few weeks later, Bill's wife read about one of our workshops and sent him along. He has now set up his own corporate hospitality organization, and his former employer is one of his key clients!

Bill's situation is a classic example of how someone can lose their perspective overnight. The reality was that nothing had actually changed about Bill. He was still loyal and committed, experienced and knowledgeable, still a good husband, but his job validated who he was, so when he lost it, he felt he had nothing left.

Our bodies are intelligent systems and communicate with us when something is wrong internally. If we are unhappy or feeling anxious or low, our intelligent physiological system will recognize and respond to our inner dialogue and feelings. If your truth is that you are anxious, bored, or stressed, your body will send you signals that there is something wrong in the form of a stress-related illness. If we don't deal with the root cause of the symptom, then the chances are the illness won't move. In Bill's case, when he got his thoughts into perspective, he felt much better and came off the medication.

Fifty and Single

Julie was an attractive, vivacious woman of 50. She looked after the home and her four teenage kids, while her lawyer husband, Tom, 51, went out to work each day. Julie's life revolved around entertaining Tom's partners and organizing the social calendar for the kids. She was a personal assistant, administrator, taxi driver, and cleaner. Her life was full, and on the whole she was happy. Sometimes she would look in the mirror and see lines appearing on her skin, but Julie was content with her face and felt secure and loved.

One day Tom announced that he had met a new woman—his 31-year-old co-worker. He said he was leaving, and Julie's world fell apart. For the first time in her life, Julie began to see in the mirror the face of an older woman; she became judgmental about her body, her self-esteem began to drop, and she started to hate herself and what she had become. She resented that she had given her world to Tom and this was how she had been repaid. She became apathetic about life; the kids were leaving home and she didn't know what to do with herself. She had no interests of her own and felt abandoned and worthless.

Julie had no real friends of her own since her friendships all revolved around entertaining her husband's partners and their wives. Julie had to start again! She had to begin to rebuild her life from scratch. I met Julie at a workshop 18 months after Tom had left.

Over the weeks and months that followed, she began to make time in her life to do the kind of things she loved, to replenish her energy and nurture her bruised soul. She began to indulge in things that she had never had time for before. She went to belly-dancing classes. She entertained some of her new friends from her evening classes. She began to write poetry, something she hadn't done since she was 19 years old. She began reading again and listening to music.

It is often a long, hard struggle to make life changes. If we really want to create interesting, fulfilling lives, it can take a bit of digging, some trial and error, and some hard work. I hope that by the time you reach the last page, you have the inspiration and courage to begin to take control of your life and make positive changes. I wish you a whole lot of sunshine—after all, it's your divine right and you deserve it.

Enjoy this book and if it helps, pass it on to a friend.

Love, Dawn xxx

Introduction

Have you ever had one of those moments where
you look in the mirror and think to yourself . . .
Who is this person? What am I truly capable of? Have
you ever thought that there must be more to life
than what you are experiencing right now? Over time,
the person in front of you may have become someone's
attentive mother or father, a loyal son or daughter, supportive
husband or wife, or a caring friend. Somehow it slipped your
notice that your needs became much less important than
everyone else's.

Where has the identity of this once vibrant person gone? Do you ever feel that the "real you" has disappeared? Do you ever feel tired, exhausted, and weighed down by the burden of your life experiences? At certain times in our lives, we can feel stuck—or as if something is missing from our lives, and everywhere we turn, there seems to be a lack of choices. When we feel like this, there is a lack of motivation; and even if we did have the energy to make some changes, we wouldn't have a clue how to go about getting started.

For some of us this feeling is momentary and may revolve around one aspect of our lives —such as relationships, work, or health; but for others it's all-consuming and it's our whole existence that we feel totally dissatisfied with. Have you ever had the feeling that somewhere deep inside you, there is a well of untapped potential—a knowing that things could be different? Maybe you've had moments when you have felt that you could do so much more . . . however, these glimpses are few and far between.

IF ONLY THINGS
HAD BEEN DIFFERENT IN YOUR LIFE

Have you ever wondered what your life could have been like had you been dealt a different hand or if you'd taken a different path? Imagine how things could have been had you been born into a different family, had you never married, never had children, or if you had a different set of life experiences—if you had been born into money, been born prettier, had a different personality, or had a more shapely body . . .

Sometimes we think if only we had more time, more money, more energy, more confidence, or different people around, life would be so much better. Some people seem to get all the breaks and get what they want out of life— and others don't. Is it simply that some people are born lucky and life is easy for them, while others are just unlucky?

Do you ever recall watching a friend or a colleague from a distance and thinking: *How do they do it? How do they get what they want out of life—regardless of their life experiences?*

What we often don't consider as we watch these people is that they may have lost their partner or their parents, gotten divorced, lost their job, lost their child, or been bankrupt; they may have been laid off or had cancer and yet they still seem to get so much out of life.

Why is it that some people get the best out of life and others don't?

WHAT'S THE MAGIC FORMULA?

Here comes the brutal truth! It's nothing magical or superhuman—with the right attitude and belief in themselves, anyone can make so much of their lives if they really decide to put their minds to it. We all know someone who has done it. We just need to observe the crazy world of showbiz and listen to the life stories of celebrities to realize that some people make it to the top in the face of adversity, or against all odds . . .

I have tremendous respect for former Spice Girl Geri Halliwell's fighting spirit. One week she is hailed as a media icon and the next the press crucify her. She never gives up, and like a phoenix from the ashes, time after time she rises again. How on earth did she get to where she is today? Was it her exceptional talent, her stunning looks, or wealthy parents? You be the judge!

Oscar winner Whoopi Goldberg's story is a fantastic testimony to the power of outstanding self-belief. Whoopi had been brought up in the Bronx, where she was repeatedly told that she would never make it in the movies because she was ugly, black, and didn't have the qualifications to get into drama school. On the night of the Oscars, Whoopi held her award high up in the air, and with tears in her eyes, she said, "Children of the world, never give up on your dream." She obviously didn't listen to anyone but her own encouraging inner voice of self-belief.

Richard Branson, a worldly entrepreneur, is dyslexic, and a teacher told him time and time again that he would never make it.

Actor Billy Connolly admitted that his father had abused him; he fought the demon drink for years, and evening after evening he got back on stage and crafted his dream of being a performer.

And can you imagine where Danny DeVito and Kylie Minogue would be if they had sat around wishing they had been a bit taller so they'd have the confidence to go on auditions!?

The bottom line is that some people just never give in; they focus on what is good about themselves and charge forward with incredible self-belief. Why do they succeed against the odds? The simple truth is that they don't dwell on the past or focus on what has gone wrong in their lives or on what they don't have. They have a belief and confidence in themselves to drive forward and to shape their lives the way they desperately want them to be—regardless of shape, size, color, creed, or background. They have a clear vision of the way they want to live their lives, and with all the determination and will in the world, they charge toward their dream. It takes a great amount of energy and an absolute will to succeed . . . especially when they are knocked around and fall down. However, they just dust themselves off and charge on again until they get to exactly where they want to be.

Something's got to change . . .

Have you contemplated recently how you would really love your life to be, or do you feel too stuck to think? Do you long for a change but don't know how to get off the treadmill or out of your rut? Do you know deep down that life could be so much better?

Secretly you know that somewhere deep inside, you have the ability to do what you would love to do, but you simply don't know how . . .

In this book I am going to take you on a journey to find out all about you—what's shaped you, what lights your fire and excites you, what you like about yourself and what you dislike, what makes you do well in life, and what continues to hold you back.

Once we work out what you think and what you believe, I will teach you some very powerful, tried-and-tested coping strategies to move you forward in your life. I'll help you build your self-confidence and self-belief, I'll teach you to be more assertive, show you how to get a handle on your emotions, and I'll help you understand why you feel and behave the way you do. I'm going to show you some really creative techniques to redesign your life so that it really is worth jumping out of bed for each morning! I am going to gently take you by the hand and work with you to show you how you can begin to make some fundamental changes, primarily about the way you feel about yourself. Then I'm going to help you begin to shape the type of life you would really love to live.

Maybe right now a feeling will click inside you and you will be desperate to move forward with this book. On the other hand, you might think it sounds like too much hard work.

You picked this book up— something made you do that. Somewhere deep inside you obviously crave some sort of change. Please make this effort, not for me but for you. Give it a try, it could be the key to a brand new way of life for you. I know this takes courage.

Your call . . . what do you have to lose?

"I am going to take you on a journey to find out all about you."

CHAPTER ONE

How Our Thoughts Create Our World

This book is primarily about our thoughts and beliefs about
ourselves and how these create and shape our reality, our lives,
and our experiences, every day of our lives.

Our thoughts affect the way we feel. They drive our motivation, enthusiasm, and well-being, and until we get a handle on them and begin to realize the impact that they have on our lives and our relationships with everyone around us, our days will continue to be shaped by chance!

Conversely, if we begin to become aware of our thoughts, then we can really improve many different aspects of our lives. We can boost our self-confidence, improve the way we feel about other people, improve our health, increase our motivation, and more. Becoming aware of what you think and believe about yourself and improving upon it can open doors to new exciting opportunities and emotions in your life . . . believe me, I've done it!

CHECK OUT THIS CONCEPT:

From our thoughts, our actions are created.
From our actions, our habits are created.
From our habits, our character is created.
From our character, our DESTINY
is created.

Every thought drives you to do something. If we do something once and get a reasonable response, whether it's a good or a bad thing, we do it again without thinking. If you do it over and over, it soon becomes a habit. Habitual behavior begins to shape your character and the way you are perceived by people around you. Whoever you have become and whatever your attitude is about life, this in turn will ultimately shape your destiny. Let me give you an example of how this theory works in practice.

'From our character our DESTINY is created.'

Claire's Story

One day when I woke up, my daughter was sick. I called the school to let her teacher know that she wouldn't be in that day. I called at 7:30 A.M. as I was about to travel to work. A lovely lady answered the phone and said, "Good morning. St Michael's Primary School. How can I help you?" I said that I was Liberty's mom and that she wasn't going to be coming to school this morning. The lady replied, "I'm really sorry, there's nobody here to take your call right now." I thought it very odd—either she has an identity crisis and didn't know she was there or she can't take a message! She told me to call back after 8:15. I called back and a man answered. Again, he wouldn't take the message and told me to call back at 8:30 A.M. when one of the office staff would be there.

As fate had it, I met Claire—the school cleaner who didn't know she was there! Like so many people, Claire dreamed of her ideal life, but her self-doubts and limiting beliefs ensured that the doors stayed firmly locked. Every Saturday night, Claire and her friend the janitor would head out to the local pub where they would discuss buying a lottery ticket that week, and what they would do with the money if they were to win. The janitor described his bright red Lamborghini and his beach house in Spain, while Claire dreamed of buying a house, taking the kids on a great vacation, and buying herself a brand new car. Unfortunately, the chances of either of them winning the lottery were virtually zero.

When I talked to Claire, I found out that she had been outgoing and popular at school, but it became apparent that when she added five and five together, she didn't get ten. At a tender age she began to develop some powerful beliefs about herself, such as that she was stupid and unintelligent. Like most dyslexic children, Claire had been resourceful; however, the academic system was not equipped to deal with children's different learning styles and multiple abilities. As a result, Claire didn't fit into the system and rebelled. How familiar does this sound?

The only way for Claire to retain any kind of self-respect was to hang out with kids who weren't doing so well at school, and before she knew it, she was 16 years old. She followed in the footsteps of her mother and took a cleaning job at the local school. She promised herself that in the future she would go to college and get some qualifications so that she could apply for an office job. Fifteen years and four kids later . . . reality kicked in fast and the office job became a pipe dream. The need for security took over, and now Claire, like so many people, found herself on the survival treadmill of life.

As we talked, I realized that Claire was bright. At the core of her being she felt that she could do so much more with her life. Having been tormented at school, however, her

> "The janitor described his bright red Lamborghini and his beach house in Spain . . ."

beliefs about her ability had paralyzed her, and she was frightened to try anything in case she failed and was found out.

I asked what she was frightened of. She replied that if, for example, she took a telephone message down incorrectly, she would be terrified of the consequences. At home, Claire handled everything like paying the bills, planning vacations, and organizing the kids. I asked her to tell me the worst thing that had happened as a result of the way she dealt with paperwork or phone calls at home, and she told me nothing ever went wrong. "If you run it all so well and efficiently at home," I said, "why can't you do it at work?"

"It's different," she replied, but couldn't explain why.

Claire wanted a new job but didn't know how to go about it. With all her responsibilities, she felt trapped and didn't know how to get out.

I made Claire a challenge. I told her that if we were to work toward one of her dreams, initially things would feel a bit awkward and maybe even scary at times. Like anything in life, once we try a new thing a few times it becomes more familiar until ultimately we don't even think about it. This was the teething process we had to go through. Claire agreed that on Monday morning she was going to take the calls that came in before 8:30 A.M. She suggested that to overcome her fear of taking down the wrong message, she would write the message down then verbally pass it on to one of the office staff.

"Claire didn't fit into the system and rebelled."

Success! After one week she was taking the messages down easily, and by the end of a month, she was confident enough to leave notes with the messages on the administrator's desk. Two months later, one of the office staff went on maternity leave, and Claire was offered a three-month contract. Now, four years later, she has a new car and takes the kids on regular summer vacations.

The moral of the story is that Claire was courageous; she challenged her beliefs about being incapable of doing the job, created a new perspective, and once she tried it, of course she could do it! Once she changed her thoughts, her actions and reactions at work changed. Her story is such a familiar one—does it ring any bells with you?

THE LIFE Tune-Up

I truly believe that once a year everyone should review their self-beliefs and habits. Each year when we encounter the knocks and bumps of life, we fall prey to believing things that can be so detrimental to our future. This process is a bit like a service or tune-up for your car. After all, we wouldn't drive a car that was using the wrong gas, operating with bad brakes, or had a flat tire. Yet we often run out of steam, run on empty, or are worn out, and there is no mechanism in place to stop us finding ourselves in bad health.

Make it your mission to read this book once a year and pass it on to anyone else you know who should be doing the same thing.

"I hope that this book can become a **self-help** bible for you."

CHAPTER TWO

As Children
We Are Perfect

Like Claire, many of us have potential that
just yearns to be tapped in to. Each and every
one of us is born with a number of fundamental and pure
characteristics that need to be satisfied to really experience
happiness in our lives.

believe that if we live out of alignment with these characteristics, we can actually move away from the unique human being that we were born to be. We become someone else, whether we are trying to be or as a result of our conditioning. In this way we can become immune to life. When we don't engage with our uniqueness or our authentic desires and aspirations, we find ourselves in a rut, and life can feel like a treadmill. In this dull existence, we lose the juice of life and can feel so out of sorts.

I believe many of us have not received fully adequate parenting, and as a result have not learned to really look after ourselves emotionally. Sometimes we feel unloved, unsupported, frightened, or needy. This is not a criticism of our parents, as they were doing the best they could in the circumstances with the knowledge and information that they had.

When we feel this way, many of us try to give our inner being a boost by overeating, overworking, or over-indulging in chocolate, drinking, drugs, sex, and other habits that do us absolutely no good. The first step to understanding who we are involves working out our truths and learning to nurture ourselves consciously and wisely. The second is about clearing negative emotional habits and behaviors that we have developed to protect ourselves as children.

It is important that we connect again with who we were as children. I believe that when we do this, we connect with our soul and our heart's desires.

As we make contact with our true feelings and needs, we find that our everyday defense mechanisms become less necessary. We start to enjoy life, let go of what doesn't work for us, and begin to welcome in the new. Then we can have emotional depth in our lives as we begin to rediscover spontaneity, innocence, fun, and joy.

I'm not suggesting here that you begin to act like a child again; however, by engaging with your inner child more often, you can bring more balance, harmony, and fulfillment into life. When we were children, we played, loved, created, and trusted so readily . . . remember what you were like when you were six years old? Think of the colors, the sights, the smells around you . . . think back to your bedroom, your interests, the friends you had, what you loved doing. Think of the people around you whom you loved being with. For most of us, at six years old we were free as a bird, unaffected by life's experiences and by the beliefs and judgments of others. At six you were you, and the world lay before you. Life was an adventure and you were free. As we grow older, we are shaped and molded by the beliefs and the expectations of everyone around us. I believe that no matter who we are and how we have been treated or affected by our life experiences, we have an authentic gift at the core of our being. The six-year-old's character lies at the heart or the core of who we are, and when we are either completely relaxed or distressed and therefore less self-conscious, we can tap in to this character again.

I often use the analogy of people being a bit like onions—just as the best part of the onion lies at the core, all our talent, truth, and potential are hidden at the heart of our accumulated layers of conditioning and life experience. These layers are our limiting beliefs about ourselves, our fears and doubts. Their job is to keep the potential firmly locked in, stopping us from making any changes that may threaten the everyday routine, and some of us have never had the opportunity, the time, or the encouragement to peel back the layers. When we are completely relaxed, the potential and the inner courage can emerge in conversation, in the things we do, or in the way we behave, revealing little glimpses of the person that we really are . . . or that we would love to become.

"Let go of what doesn't work."

SELF-EXPRESSION

As children we have a deep need to express who we really are. Each and every one of us has a unique form of self-expression. Some people are artistic, some people love to tell jokes, for some people it's music—or just whatever comes naturally. So often young children are told not to show off or not to be silly. I think it's so sad that parents often don't realize they are shutting out true expression when they dismiss or criticize their children, and expect them to do as they have done rather than blossom into the person they really deserve to be.

I can remember when I was six years old, walking to school with my friend Colin. I would ballet dance and try to fly to school. I did it because I felt the urge and I was free as a bird. One day people began to make fun of me; they thought I was odd, and so I stopped. That was the moment when I began to suppress my creative urges and became aware that other people were not comfortable with my self-expression. How often do we stifle this creative urge as kids or even as adults?

Interestingly, though, we might think that we have lost it, but self-expression never actually leaves us. Can you remember being at a wedding, having a few glasses of wine, and then hearing the band strike up? You are sitting in anticipation of someone making a move onto

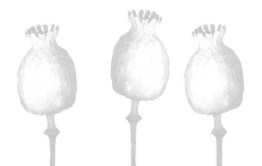

the dance floor so that you can get up and strut your stuff! Has this happened to you? Or at a karaoke night, you feel that you could do much better than the person who is singing and the urge is there to get up and sing like you have never sung before; however, the fear paralyzes you and you tell yourself that you can't do it because you might make a fool of yourself.

I know personally that with a few glasses of wine and the right people around me, my self-expression and creativity go wild! I feel most like being me when I'm relaxed and happy. When I'm being me, it's the best feeling in the world . . . however, some people don't like it, and that can be tough! After a great weekend with friends, Monday morning inevitably arrives, and it's amazing how we can tuck our self-expression away and once again become who we are expected to be.

Let's Do a Self-Expression Checkup!

What did you love to do as a child?

Think back and record your thoughts and feelings in your journal.

Dress up	Do adventure sports	Camp	Play football
Read	Climb	Play with friends	Play in the woods
Sing	Build things	Dance	Play in water
Make things	Think	Watch movies	Have pillow fights
Bake cakes	Collect things	Ride bikes	Play with animals
Joke			

Who stopped you expressing yourself fully and why?

Parents	Kids	Church	Grandparents
Friends	Family	Bosses	Partners

Who was it for you?

When you are feeling really relaxed, how do you like to express yourself?

Singing	Dancing	Being playful	Performing
Laughing	Crying	Storytelling	

What is it for you . . . what lurks deep within you?

What feels natural to you that might not sit so easily with your family or friends?

VULNERABILITY

Our vulnerable self is the emotional core of our being. This part of us carries all our deepest feelings and is sensitive, loving, and easily hurt and frightened. This part of us reacts to everything that is happening in our world, weighing whether it feels safe and loved or threatened, rejected, or abandoned. It needs a great deal of love, nurturing, and reassurance. Often our vulnerable child has been wounded through life experiences, and it may be in need of healing or professional help or attention.

Sometimes when we have been hurt on a deep level, we learn to protect ourselves by keeping our true feelings suppressed and often locked away. This part of us shuts down the emotions to ensure that we don't become anxious or upset or hurt in any way. These mechanisms help us to function in the world, but by suppressing the essential part of our being, we can often cut ourselves off from the source of joy that could be just what we need to heal and feel real joy in our lives again.

LOVE AND TRUST

As children we want desperately to be loved and to love in return. Sometimes as adults, love is not as abundant in our lives as it should be, leaving us alone, lonely, or unhappy. I think love is the most amazing human emotion, and when we find it with another person or even with ourselves, it's the most potent force in the world. Sometimes we need to develop trust in ourselves and in others. Being unable to trust is painful.

From every life experience we go through, we need to learn our lessons—otherwise we continually repeat bad patterns. When we live and learn, we can begin to build a new life, confident in the knowledge that we can survive whatever we go through.

I have dedicated so much of this book to learning how to love and respect yourself, and when you begin to take these principles on board, you can create boundaries to ensure that you are protected and safe. The biggest challenge about not trusting is that a wonderful new future where you are free could be just around the corner, and if you decide not to explore this possibility, an essential part of your being will be cut off from something that could bring you much joy in your life.

> "I think love is the most amazing human emotion, and when we find it with another person or even with ourselves, it's the most potent force in the world."

When love and trust are breached, there can be tremendous pain and often devastating consequences in our lives. If we love and trust deeply and these abilities are lost, for some people the distance is too far to travel to repair the wounds. If you are the person who wounds, you may get off lightly—for a while. A wounded person can appear to others as a sensitive, bruised individual or the type who is always bad-tempered, bitchy, or distant. So many people have been wounded by partners, bosses, family, or friends, and have put up a defense mechanism like a tough shield that doesn't let anyone in and won't allow them to be hurt again. They might be perceived as being difficult; however, in reality it's just that they are protecting themselves from being hurt again.

said, "Tell me the truth, Mary, if you could get over the hurt, wouldn't you like someone to love you again?" Her eyes welled up. I could see the pain on her face of all these years of resentment and anger that had turned into bitterness, and the irony is that the only person who was suffering from her venomous emotions was Mary, not her ex or her best friend.

At the end of the session, Mary signed up for my workshop but she never did turn up. I felt sad about this, as it was a chance for her to get over her pain. I often meet people who have had a bad experience in life, and as a result have given up faith in themselves and in life. Hold on tight and keep reading, because we do have remedies, I promise!

Mary's Story

In a short session to promote a *Zest for Life* workshop, Mary said that she didn't think it was necessary to be vulnerable. She had been divorced for 20 years. Mary's husband had gone off with her best friend, and she took great pride in telling me that she hated men and warned all young girls "not to get involved." I listened to what she had to say, and then I looked right into her eyes and

"Her eyes welled up. I could see the pain on her face . . ."

VULNERABILITY CHECK

Can you remember how it felt to be vulnerable? Think back to a time when you felt really happy, open, and honest, showing your vulnerability. How did it feel? Circle the words below that strike a chord.

Safe	Comfortable	Warm	Wonderful
Honest	Soft	Alive	Loved
Adventurous	Open	Spontaneous	Just right
Trusting	How it should be	On fire	

Record what you think and feel in your journal.

What is it that scares you about opening up again?

Getting hurt again	Getting it wrong again	Not being able to trust	Not being me
Being a fool again	It will never be the same	Not being able to forgive	

What is it for you?

Record your feelings in a journal.

Now reflect on the positive lessons you learned from your painful past experience—dig deep for this one.

Do any of the following apply to you?

Better to love than not	Learn and move on	I am worth loving	I am resilient
Love is the greatest gift	I can always bounce back	I always listen to my instincts	

What was it for you? Could you recover if you did open up and something happened again?

Record your thoughts and feelings in a journal.

What do you stand to lose if you don't open up again?

Never loving again	Being lonely	Being isolated	True happiness
Never knowing	Never trusting again	Being sad	True trust
True love	Always wondering *what if . . . ?*		

What do you feel?
Record your feelings in a journal.

FUN AND PLAY

As children, having fun and playing are a major part of our lives. When I watch and listen to my daughter, I realize that she is intent on having as much fun and play as she can possibly have in her little life. I remember one morning heading off to work when she said to me, "Mom, what do you do for a job?" I said, "Well, I'm a kind of teacher." Her eyes sparkled, and with a big smile she said, "Oh, are you a somersault teacher?" To an eight-year-old child, a PE teacher was obviously her idea of the most exciting teaching job around . . . and she thought I had it!

When we are kids, our imagination runs wild—we love to play, create, and have fun. But as we grow up, responsibility kicks in and we forget all about playing. Then routine takes over, and before we know it, life is all too serious, so much so that when we have our own children so many of us forget how to play with them.

I remember Liberty playing with some big paintbrushes and paints, coloring in some shapes I had drawn. Sitting over her as she painted, I was making sure that she didn't cross any of the lines with her paintbrush. Then I realized what I was doing—playing is not about being a perfectionist or getting things right; it's about having fun.

So many people who come to my workshops tell me that they aren't creative; they say they can't draw, can't sing, can't play an instrument, can't do a mosaic on a plant pot . . . why not? Because they want it to be perfect. If they can't paint like Picasso or Monet, they won't do it! And even if they can paint, they don't make the time anymore. I have some brushes and paints and regularly play at painting. I wouldn't go around showing everyone what I do, but for me it's fun and sometimes a lovely, creative challenge. I mosaic everything that moves, because I love getting my hands covered in grout, and I love

"Don't just think about it: pick up the phone . . ."

smashing up tiles. When did you last do something just for the fun of it? If you do something fun and creative every day, it becomes a habit, but if life becomes too serious and grown-up, the first thing to go is the fun stuff.

Don't fret, though . . . it's as simple to reintroduce into our lives as it was to lose it!

FUN FRIDAYS

My friend Mhairi and her husband, Andrew, make every Friday night Fun Friday night. I remember that even when Mhairi was very pregnant, she still kept up the challenge. Each week she and her husband would take turns choosing a new venue for a night out—they'd go to shows, comedy clubs, karaoke bars, or restaurants. When the new baby eventually came along, Fun Fridays continued . . . they have a fantastic relationship. So many of us give up when the kids come along. Setting aside a particular day in the week can quickly establish a new routine.

PAJAMA DAYS

Another fun thing to do with the family is to have a pajama day once a month. My friends Christine and Michael and their kids spend whole days in their PJs doing things like eating chocolate ice cream, tickling, watching movies, cuddling . . . all in their great big bed! The kids love it, and it is a great inexpensive, stress-free family day.

When was the last time you had a good laugh? Who could you catch up with to have a giggle with? Don't just think about it; pick up the phone and make a date today!

EXERCISE
What do you like to do to have fun?

Dancing	Laughing	Tricks	Magic
Tickling	Singing	Comedy	Games
Pillow-fighting	Water fights	Sports	Socializing
Making things	Jokes		

LIST WHAT YOU LOVE
What creative or fun activity have you always thought about trying but have never had the courage to do? Could you try it at home just for fun?

Karaoke	Salsa dancing	Painting	Writing poetry
Writing a novel	Making things	Stand-up comedy	Singing
Playing a musical instrument			

What would you love?

INTUITION

Intuition, gut feeling, and *sixth sense* are all terms that we use to describe the messenger system that we connect with when we feel something on a deep level. We know, whether we choose to admit it or not, when something is right or wrong for us. As children we are tuned in to our intuition; we can sense things, and at an early age we begin to act upon our instincts.

For example, when you were a child playing in the playground at school and someone came up and kicked you in the shin, there's no way you would be friends with a person like that. It would be very easy for you to make this decision. As adults, however, people hurt us, abuse us, put us down, and take us for granted, and on a deep level we know that we should make a change in our personal or our working life. But the thought of rocking the boat or upsetting anyone stops us from saying what needs to be said or doing what needs to be done.

If we can access our intuition, then we can be free and fly with life; we can cruise along doing what is right for us, following our heart's desires. My firm belief is that so many people don't know how to access their intuition because they have become so rigidly shaped in their lives and they haven't stopped to ask what they would really love to be doing . . . ever.

At one point in my life when faced with a very difficult decision —probably the toughest decision of my life—I believed that I didn't know what I should do. Fear had taken over and I'd buried my instincts so deeply that I felt like a deer caught in the headlights—startled and stuck. I just didn't know which way to turn.

When my female friends have a challenge, they talk it over with me time and time again. Usually I can clearly see the solution to their problem from the outside. If we let our emotion and fear of dealing with the consequences of a situation take over so that we are constantly churning the situation over in our mind, we can't access our intuition. Then we might have one too many to drink, and the truth and the intuition surfaces, as does the courage to make the necessary changes.

Next day the sun rises, the fear sets, nothing changes, and the solution is buried until the next time.

SECURITY AND BELONGING

When we are born into this world, we have a deep need to belong. Within hours of our birth, we are given a name and registered to a place and a parent. When we belong, we feel safe, we feel loved, we feel that we have the security to survive. We need to feel love and to know where our home is. When children don't have that luxury and perhaps find themselves in foster care at that early age, the struggle to belong begins.

As adults, the thought of being alone can be terrifying, so people remain in relationships or connected to families who abuse and mistreat them. Part of their being desperately wants to be free, but the fear of being alone or coping on their own keeps them in a place where they are unhappy, frustrated, and sad. In this book I will give you the opportunity to build your freedom within a relationship; I'll also help you find the courage to get out of one if it's absolutely necessary, or learn some techniques that will enable you to enhance your relationship and ensure that you get back in control.

NEED FOR SECURITY

It is a practical reality that every time we make a decision about our future, the monthly rent or mortgage are often the greatest considerations in whether we go for our dreams or not.

EXERCISE

Light a candle and sit with your journal/sketch pad and just begin to write some answers to these questions. It may seem like you are scribbling nonsense at first—don't judge; just observe what comes up for you.

1. On a deep level, what do you feel you are capable of, and what would you love to do? At this stage, you are only having a little look at what lies at your core. Don't be afraid to just play with the idea—it's only a daydream, so write it down.

2. Instinctively, what do you know you should do to make life better at work or personally? Be aware here of any physiological reactions that you may have, pain in your chest, tummy, tears—they all symbolize some sort of uneasiness in your life.

3. What people do you know you should let go of or spend less time with in your life?

- People who take all your energy
- People who are constantly negative
- People who put you down
- People who squash your ideas
- People who use you
- People who don't support you
- People who dump on you

As we get older, we buy bigger homes and take on higher mortgages; the bigger the mortgage, the less space for creativity, change, fun, and risk-taking. Wouldn't it be great if we made the compromise to live in a smaller house and did what we loved to do each day? That would make perfect sense to me . . . but what would the neighbors or your family say?

So many people have safety and security mixed up with money. Most of us to some degree or another are frightened about not having enough money. We feel somehow that money offers us security. We always believe that if we had more money, we would feel more secure. This is a myth. Money makes the inside child feel really safe, however, so often money is not what is truly taking care of all of the inner child's needs. The need for security can crush our creativity, destroy our dreams, paralyze our imagination, and leave us in a place where we are left with huge feelings of emptiness. It can leave us feeling that we have no choices . . . but it doesn't have to be that way. In Exercise 7 on the Mechanics of the Brain, we will look at how we can recover our inner creativity, and begin to see the importance of being creative in recovering joy and happiness in our lives.

Stewart and Mariesha's Story

I'm writing this book in an apartment overlooking the sea at the marina in Almerimar in Spain. The apartment is owned by Stewart and Mariesha. Mariesha was a lawyer in London, and Stewart was a golf professional running a busy shop and practice in southwest England. One day they decided they wanted a change, so they toured around Europe for six months then moved to Spain. In the last 18 months, they have bought, renovated, and sold one or two little properties. They have enough money to get by, they go to the beach often, eat out a lot, and have acquired a menagerie of pets. They fit in well here and are having a ball. They now have freedom and happiness and a fraction of the money they used to make, but they are loving life.

At home, people couldn't understand how they could do such an irresponsible thing. I believe that because of people's deep need for security, they are fearful for themselves and for other people when they take risks. In Mariesha and Stewart's case, there was no great risk involved.

Be honest with yourself. Do any of the following ring true with you?

• I need to be in a relationship, so I put up with relationships that are disrespectful.
• I need to be loved, so I never risk speaking up for myself.
• I don't want to speak my mind at work in case I lose my job.
• I want to be more authentic, but what if people reject me?
• I want to live my dream, but how could I pay the mortgage?
• I hate my job but feel it's too risky to make a change.
• My passion will never be realized because I don't want to give up this standard of living.
• I know I should get out of the relationship I'm in, but I don't want to be on my own.

EXERCISE 1
Here are some BIG questions for you to answer: What are you frightened of doing/saying
in case it upsets your security?

Changing jobs   Getting divorced
Moving to another part of the world   Getting married
Setting up your own business   Saying no to someone
Having a child   Expressing how you truly feel
Leaving someone you have fallen out of love with

What is it for you? Record what you found here in your journal. If you can, write about how you feel.

EXERCISE 2
If the mortgage or the rent weren't considerations, what would you love to do
with your life? Dream a bit!

Be self-employed   Move abroad   Live alone   Have more children
Get divorced   Get married   Buy a classic car   Work part-time
Be free   Travel   Give up work
Buy a house in the sun   Move in with my partner Take the issue to a higher power

What is it for you?

Well done! We'll come back to this and
explore what you are truly afraid of or what's
really holding you back later on in the book.

CHAPTER THREE

The Stepping-Stones
on Our Life Journey

In the last chapter, we explored our fundamental
childhood characteristics such as self-expression,
vulnerability, fun and play, intuition, and security that we
play out from a very early age. As we grow older, many of
us feel out of touch with one or more of these elements and
as a result, we might feel that something is missing in our lives.

When you aren't doing what you love or following the dictates of your soul, then you will feel totally out of alignment with your authentic self. If you spend your whole life doing what everyone else wants rather than what you would love to do, then you are *doing* life, not *living* life! So how on earth did you get to where you are today?

I often use the analogy of life as a great big river. We are born on the left bank of the river and our life ambition is to head over to the right bank. On the right bank there is a great canvas with an image of how your ideal health would be, how your ideal partner would be, your ideal daily work, your ideal waist size, or your ideal bust size!

Our challenge is that on our journey to the right bank we must cross some huge stepping-stones, each one of these stones offering us a life experience that will shape us as human beings. Depending on how we cope with each experience, the outcome determines whether or not we reach that final destination. At times it will be easy to travel from one stepping-stone to the next, and at other times the distance from one stone to the next might seem too great—the energy required to travel may be too much and the threat of the muddy waters might leave you questioning whether to bother with the next move. Even if you do summon up the energy, there is always the impending risk of falling into the river!

From the moment we arrive on this planet, we are born into the hands of another human being who, with the best intentions in the world, will shape us, protect us, be responsible for us, love us the only way they know how. The stepping-stones begin . . .

Stepping-Stone Number 1

WORRIERS OR WARRIORS

Watch toddlers as they arrive at a swing park full of swings, see-saws, and merry-go-rounds—they always seem to spot the high jungle gym and slide and make a run for it! As a parent or guardian of these kids, we are naturally concerned. Instinctively so many of us would call, "Be careful." Unaware and oblivious, at this very early age the child thinks *danger*. While this is a natural reaction, often parents who are trying to protect their children actually stifle their risk-taking abilities and adventurous spirit. When we feel fearful for our children, we impress our fear upon them, and as a result they absorb it and feel fearful and worry about things they want to do in their lives.

LIBERTY CLIMBING THE ROCKS

Outside my house there are some huge rocks that stretch down to the beach. They are pretty easy to climb. From the path, the drop down to the beach is about 12 feet. Once I was at the beach with my daughter, Liberty, who was then three years old. I was almost halfway down the rocks when I realized that my little person wasn't with me! When I looked back, there she was, standing like a little statue. I asked her why she hadn't followed me. She said, "I can't do it, Mommy." I went back up to the top and explained that it was safe to climb down the rocks and if she told herself *I can* instead of *I can't,* her legs would become unstuck! She began to repeat "I can, I can, I can!" and began climbing down. She did it!

If we are encouraged at an early age to challenge our fears, things become easier for us in later life. Were you encouraged to be a worrier or a warrior?

Stepping-Stone Number 2

AUTHENTIC YOU

At three or four, a toddler's character is developing. This is a wonderful age where we begin to see a child's creativity unspool. We find out what they like and what they don't. Their imagination is running wild and the world is their oyster.

The most important things in the child's world are making friends, playing, eating, and having fun! At this age, a bright green painted triangle can represent an angel or a tractor, and nobody would ever question it. Self-expression is coming to the fore, and the child begins to display unique character traits. The child is generally accepted unconditionally by its parents and friends, and at this tender age, one of the toughest hurdles of their little lives is just around the corner.

At five years old, the child enters the world of academia, where if you add five and five together and you don't get ten you might just begin to develop some damaging lifelong beliefs. If, however, you add five and five together and you do actually get ten, you have a whole different set of beliefs! This is the place where so much of your own self-perception will be formed.

Fortunately, schools are beginning to acknowledge different forms of intelligence, allowing children to be recognized as unique and individual, validating them for their qualities, and honoring their unique learning styles.

I remember choosing my daughter's elementary school. One of the prerequisites for me was that they weren't going to force her into academia, instead allowing her to evolve according to whatever her own talents were. I was so encouraged by the outcome. I know many people who have done well in their lives and they weren't in any shape or form academic. The opposite applies, too! What worries me more than anything is the huge number of people who spent their time at school bobbing somewhere in the middle and never really pushed themselves because they weren't particularly bright, but certainly weren't dim. I know that many of these people have moments in their lives when they think that they could do so much more . . .

Stepping-Stone Number 3

THE BIKE

Do you remember riding your bike for the first time? Can you remember jumping onto the steel frame as people were standing by in anticipation? Can you remember feeling the support and encouragement as people cheered for you? As you jump on for the first time, the frame wobbles, you fall off, you skin your knees and elbows, and you are bleeding!

I bet your bottom dollar that never for a moment would anyone ever say to you, "You have failed, now don't get on that bike again." It's interesting how the psychology of teaching children to ride bikes works. There is total unconditional support for you to succeed. Your parents want you to be able to ride your bike. As a child you want to keep up with the other kids so you need to be able to ride your bike no matter what happens—if you break a limb, if you're bleeding from head to toe, everyone encourages you to get up and try again. They promise you that they will always support you, even if you fall off a hundred times!

"Do you remember riding your bike for the first time?"

Can you imagine if this was how we were consistently treated in our lives? The harsh reality is that beyond learning to ride the bike, often the support network disappears and we find that other people are too frightened in their own lives to support and encourage us to take risks in ours.

Stepping-Stone Number 4

CHILDREN MAKING ADULT CHOICES

At the age of 13, children are asked to begin considering what they would like to do for a career. Can you remember thinking about what you were going to do for the rest of your life? How bizarre this concept is. Your ideas are starting to form, the image on the canvas is beginning to take shape, you know at this age what you're quite good at and what you're not good at, and what you are and aren't interested in.

I was passionate about becoming an actress; however, my father had a completely different plan for me. Dad reminded me that I wasn't pretty enough and couldn't sing well enough to become an actress—his vision of an actress was Doris Day. He was protective of me and wanted me to have a secure future, so he stopped me from taking all the arts subjects at school that I found interesting and easy to do.

Instead, he guided me onto the academic route of becoming a lawyer: He felt it was a safer option for me. Dad died when I was 16 years old. I couldn't concentrate, and I abandoned the goal of becoming a lawyer; it wasn't mine anyway. I started working in administration, and until I was 26, I hadn't realized that I'd buried the dream of becoming an actress.

I wonder how many children are steered away from passion and interests in the direction of security at this tender age?

At 13, we still have so much creativity and imagination, and unfortunately, this is where the image on the canvas of our ideal passion or daily work can be rubbed out forever. Once we start work, even if we promise ourselves that the job will only be for a few years, the security of a regular salary gets to us. Often we don't want to risk change and can find ourselves in a job that doesn't interest us for years!

Stepping-Stone Number 5

UNCOMFORTABLE COMFORT ZONES

This is the most comfortable stepping-stone: It feels safe, there's a lovely furry carpet on it, a nice big TV to watch the soaps, a fridge full of beer or wine, and on the whole it feels pretty good. The canvas in the distance is a little misty in parts and in other parts it's pretty clear. On the whole you're happy here. You might have a partner, and maybe you have kids. You have just enough money to cover the monthly rent or mortgage, and you have a clear idea of how much spending money you have for little luxuries every month. You go to work every day, come home, cook supper, watch a bit of TV, and look after the kids—if you have them. You go to bed then do the same thing the next day. You long for the weekends, and Fridays can't come quickly enough!

One night when you are sitting in front of the TV, something comes onto the screen, and for a split second your imagination is sparked. The routine of your daily life disappears, and the canvas on the right bank of the river is filled with a vibrant image of how you would love your life to be, every day. You see yourself happy, fulfilled, and excited about the future. You think for a moment about how you would love to do this thing—it may involve a change of job, career, or lifestyle. In that split second you feel that anything is possible; your dreams are awakened and you feel free to play with all the possibilities in life. You want to take the chance.

In that moment, you may turn to your partner or friend, and with spontaneous enthusiasm share your thoughts . . . and their immediate response is, "Don't be silly. How on earth do you think we will be able to pay the bills or care for the kids if you were to do that?" Your heart sinks, the image on the canvas fades, and in a fraction of a second your dream is taken away. Then you think to yourself, *You're right, what was I thinking of?*

For some of us, it's not our partner who sabotages our dream. We are more than capable of doing it for ourselves. As we imagine how our lives could be, a voice in our head begins to remind us how it would be too big a risk, we probably wouldn't succeed, and that we shouldn't be so silly.

Stepping-Stone Number 6

YOUR 80TH BIRTHDAY

This is the final stepping-stone—the one closest to your dreams and aspirations. This is the stepping-stone of your 80th birthday that you'll reach only if you are very lucky!

• How many 80-year-olds do you know?

What will you be able to say about the life that you have lived? Will you be able to talk about a fulfilled, interesting life, or just about your existence?

What risks do you think you'll wish, in hindsight, that you had taken? What places do you think you will wish you had traveled to? What college course will you wish you had taken? What situations will you wish you had changed?

How much potential do you really have but have never realized? How often when people die or when we hear about people with terminal illnesses do we say, "From today things are going to change. I am going to take the bull by the horns!" The days pass by, the fight fades, and months pass. The ideas disappear, one year passes, and nothing changes. Has this ever happened to you?

This book is about listening to the desires of your heart and soul. It's about showing you some very powerful coping strategies to help you build your confidence to such a level that you feel free to make some fundamental changes in the way you think and feel each day.

If you have been abused, bullied, divorced, widowed, laid off, homeless, addicted, depressed, fired, ill, stuck in a rut, or frightened . . . this book is for you. Or it will benefit your mother, sister, daughter, brother, aunt, or friends. There are going to be times when we are bereaved, when we are ill, when we are going through menopause—times when we feel it's all too much and it's not worth the effort to lift ourselves up again. Life is tough, and there is no getting away from it; however, we do have choices. Keep reading. I will show you how you can begin to feel different about yourself, and this book will offer you the tools and techniques to change even the most negative, cynical mind-set. Please give yourself this chance; do the exercises and practice them . . . they work, I promise.

CHAPTER FOUR

What's Shaping Your Life?

In this chapter, we're going to do an exercise to remind you of just how important and significant you are as a human being. We often consider everyone else's needs before our own, especially if we have children. If our parents have sacrificed their lives for their children, then chances are that we will do the same. If you don't break the habit, the danger is that your kids are going to do exactly what you have done in your life.

The Airplane Story

This story has a ring of truth for me. A loving mother was traveling in an airplane with her twin daughters, whom she loved equally. The pilot announced that they were about to encounter some turbulence. He said that the cabin pressure had dropped drastically and the oxygen masks were about to fall. (Anyone who has traveled on a plane will know that when the oxygen masks drop, parents are advised to put their own masks on first and then tend to their children.)

In this case, the woman couldn't decide which child to help out first. In her panic, without stabilizing either of her daughters' masks, she suffocated and died, and as a result, her two daughters did, too.

The moral of the story is that if you do not look after *you*, what on earth have you got to offer everyone around you? If you are stressed, burnt out, and exhausted, or if you have no interest in life, what do you have to offer your friends, partner, or children?

This is an amazing world, full of possibilities to explore and experience. You deserve to do so many things, but if you don't think you deserve to put yourself first once in a while, or feel that it would be selfish to do what you want to do, then you are in grave danger of living life on the treadmill and getting to 80 with a whole bunch of regrets. It hurts, but it's true. Keep reading—we can sort it out!

Don't get me wrong, I'm not going to encourage you to leave your partner, take up with a wild man or woman, and travel the world in a camper van. I'm talking about being heard—expressing your wants and desires for vacations, a new line of work,

---

EXERCISE 1
STOP

In preparation for this exercise, you will need a photo of yourself as a little girl or boy of about five years old. Don't do this exercise without it—it will not have the same impact if you just imagine. Now look into the eyes of this child, remember what it felt like to be him or her. Remember the spirit of this little girl or boy, look at their lovely little teeth, their skin, their hair. As you look into the eyes of this little person, ask yourself: *If I were this child's parent, what would I want for her/him?* Ask yourself one question at a time.

- How would you encourage them in their lives?
- What would you think they deserve in this life?
- How would you want their life to be?

- How should they be treated emotionally?
- How could you protect/nurture them?
- What do they need in their life right now?

taking a break from time to time—everything you deserve in this life.

How did you feel doing this exercise? It's perfectly natural to feel emotional. It reveals the real you at your core, the you that was pure and unaffected by life experiences. This will give you a connection with your truth and show you your importance and relevance as a human being.

STOP

Always be aware of the inner voice that will tell you immediately why you shouldn't have all of the above and why it's silly to be doing this exercise, since nothing can change. Your thought processes have been ingrained over years, so your automatic responses will come up. That's okay—however, feel free to record what you feel you would love to do or say to meet the needs of the child in you, even if you can't see any conceivable way of making changes right now. This is a process, and it will take time to work through it—try to just let go as you begin to rediscover your authentic needs and desires.

UNCOVERING WHAT YOU BELIEVE ABOUT YOURSELF

In this exercise, we are going to find out what you really believe about yourself. As I've said from the beginning of this book, what you think about *you* is what determines your life. In the next few exercises, we'll identify why your life is shaping up the way it is right now.

So many of your thoughts and beliefs are a result of experiences from your past. Once a year we should do a "thoughts detox" to question how we are thinking, and keep our lives on track. Remember Claire's story—she believed she wasn't capable or intelligent, but the way she looked after the house and four kids and worked at two jobs was pretty amazing! When we changed the way Claire thought about herself, she began

"This is an **amazing** world, full of possibilities to **explore** and **experience**"

STOP

I would like you to be gentle with yourself here, and also to be aware of the voice inside your head that will remind you how you couldn't possibly say anything so positive or optimistic about yourself. Please just ignore this voice, and don't be afraid of who is going to read your responses—do them in pencil. Check as many of the following as you can to reveal what you feel about yourself on a deep level. Look at the photo of your little self and ask yourself what his/her true qualities are . . .

I am capable	I am fun	I am creative	I am resourceful
I am intelligent	I am artistic	I am affectionate	I deserve the best
I am optimistic	I am adventurous	I am pretty	I am worth loving
I am positive	I am interesting	I am attractive	I deserve respect
I am natural	I am powerful	I am funny	I am well
I am honest	I deserve honesty	I am happy	I am energetic
I am loyal	I am smart	I am bright	I am fulfilled
I am sensitive	I am flexible	I am passionate	I am loving

to do things differently and then her life began to change . . . now it's your turn!

THE MENTOR

For this next exercise, I would like you to introduce an imaginary mentor—someone who will support you with whatever decisions you need to make in your life and always act in your best interests. This person is someone who loves you unconditionally, someone who believes in you and would want the best for you in every situation.

In my case my mentor is my Aunt Margaret — she believes I'm the best thing since sliced bread! Whenever I need the courage to do something new, I imagine her response in my head, anticipate how she would react to the situation, and I go for it! Your mentor can be someone who is alive or someone who is

dead; he or she can be someone you know or someone you perhaps aspire to be like. If you are really struggling, use me—or if you like, feel free to use my Aunt M!

Now go back to the exercise above, and anything you haven't checked, imagine the voice of your mentor and hear their response about you. If they challenge you and say that they think you've got it, check it. Go on, have another try.

If you managed to check a number of the items above, well done! It's amazing how we can find our qualities and talents when we dig deep. Imagine if you were to think these things about your life every day—can you imagine how different it would be?

Later on in the book you will need to come back to this section to remind

WHAT SHAPED YOUR LIFE?

Now check the sentences below, which reflect the way that you feel from day to day at this point in your life. This time, check as many as you can.

I am ill	I am without direction	I am negative	I don't deserve a good job
I am lost	I am unattractive	My life is out of control	I feel empty
I have no time	I feel judgmental	I feel oversensitive	I feel fat
I am a gossip	I am at a dead end	I feel stuck	I am terrified
I am lazy	I am sad	I am too busy	I am exhausted
I am powerless	I am critical	I feel guilty	I am stupid
I am not bright	I don't deserve love	I can't say no	I don't deserve respect

yourself of these positive qualities. If you didn't manage to check many, that's okay—let's just keep working through the exercises. Things will get better later, I promise.

Time for the brutal truth again! Whatever you have just checked reveals the standard and quality of your life right now. If you have checked most of the statements, your life will feel overbearing and heavy. If you have checked half or less, there are things that need attention. Whether you like it or not, this is how you think every day, without even giving it a second thought. These thoughts will be determining outcomes, feelings, emotions, motivation, and enthusiasm. They will determine how you behave with other people. This is how people see you, and this is what seeps through your pores at interviews, at meetings, with friends, with family. Until you begin to change these thoughts, NOTHING IS GOING TO CHANGE.

Now I would like you to go back to the top of the page and question each and every

one of them again, this time slowly. As you question them, hear the voice of your mentor. If your mentor, you, or your best friend would challenge what you have checked about you, then cross the check mark out.

Often in my workshops when people do this exercise, beautiful women say that they are unattractive; people say they are out of control, yet they are at my workshop taking control; they say they are powerless, yet in the previous exercise they say they are powerful; they say they are negative when all they do is express an opposing viewpoint to their partners. Really question your answers rationally. How much of this thinking has become habitual, and how much have you developed as a result of the knocks and bumps that you have experienced in your life? Try to detach your emotions and see what happens. How many of these check marks can you cross out?

CHAPTER FIVE

Understanding the Power of the Mind

In the last exercise, hopefully you began to realize just what sort of thoughts you are having each day. By becoming aware of them, you begin to see why perhaps your life isn't going quite the way YOU want it to go. Until you work on these thought processes and begin to change them (I'll show you how to do that later in the book), nothing in your life is going to change.

In the last exercise, you highlighted only a tiny fraction of your thought processes. Neuroscientists have identified that each day we have a staggering 70,000 thoughts, each of them determining the actions and the habits we have developed in our lives. And in turn, each of these thoughts is driving us to live and behave in a certain way. These are our conscious thoughts; we are blissfully unaware of what goes on in our subconscious mind.

$\frac{1}{8}$ conscious mind this is what we project to the world

$\frac{7}{8}$ sub-conscious mind our reality is shaped here

The illustration above shows an image of the mind as an iceberg. The piece of ice that we see is only a tiny reflection of the whole. Underneath the surface, the iceberg stretches for miles under the ocean, hidden like our subconscious. The tip of the iceberg, our conscious mind, is what we project to the rest of the world; it's the language and the thoughts we have each day.

This is the part that is responsible for thinking on our feet, making decisions, saying the right thing, and generally functioning in the world. The subconscious mind, however, is the place where our inner life is lived out, and usually we are unaware of just how much is going on in there.

CONSCIOUS THOUGHTS

Our conscious thoughts are the thoughts we have when we have to think on our feet. For example, let's imagine one day your alarm doesn't go off on time, then you debate whose fault it was with your partner for not setting the alarm properly, you then head to work, and as you do you get stuck in a traffic jam. You arrive at work a little late, your blood pressure goes up, and you begin to feel the start of a very bad day!

As you walk into the office, your regional manager has decided to "drop in for the day." As he turns to you he says, "Good morning, how are you today?" Your conscious mind scrambles together, "I'm very well, sir, and how are you?" Underneath the surface of your emotions there is turmoil; however, the face you paint on reflects something completely different. Have you ever painted the face on and said that you're fine, when really underneath you know you aren't?

SUBCONSCIOUS THOUGHTS

Our subconscious thoughts are the deep-seated beliefs that drive our conscious thoughts, and often we aren't actually aware of them. In the last exercise, you may have revealed thoughts you have about yourself that you weren't aware of. These are the ones that you need to bring into your conscious mind if you want to make changes in your life. Here are a few examples.

Do you have to think about how to drive?
Do you think about how to ride a bike?
Do you think about what side of bed to get out of each day?
Do you think about your morning routine?
Do you travel the same way to work each day?
Do you buy the same newspaper each day?

Probably all these things have become a habit, so you don't actually think about how you do them. Are you an absolute creature of habit, stuck in your ways, trapped by your rigid thoughts and beliefs, or can you easily change to ensure that you sample everything life has to offer?

THE LIGHT SWITCH

In my house there is a tall closet where I store all my clothes. There is a light inside the closet, and it's really high up. When the light-bulb blows, I repeatedly go back into the closet and switch the switch on before I change the bulb. I then have to fumble around in the dark, and this can continue for weeks! I laugh at myself every time it happens. This just shows how my reactions and habits are deeply ingrained.

Our subconscious thoughts are our habitual thoughts; they have been ingrained in us. I always smile when an old neighbor comes over to visit. When he talks about his friends and family, he always defines them by how clean they are, and as we chat he must mention the words *clean* and *immaculate* at least ten times. Obviously as a child he learned the old cliché "Cleanliness is next to godliness" ingrained into him by his mother (an immaculate woman), and this is what drives his perceptions of people.

I had dinner with a charming friend recently. He is handsome, gentle, and incredibly wealthy, and has so much to offer the right woman. Over dinner we talked of his personal situation and how he'd been on his own for five years. He defined himself as gray, fat, and old. If he perceives himself this way, he isn't going to meet anyone; if he does, he won't feel worthy because of his self-perception. I'm convinced that he isn't aware of what he is saying and how often he is saying it.

THE GREMLINS

My good friend Julie Kay calls these self-critical thoughts our "gremlins." You will recognize these as the persistent negative voices that play around in your head and override any positive thought or ambition that you may have. The gremlins tell you how you can't do things, and how you aren't good enough—all the things you should never say to yourself and certainly not to the gorgeous child of five or six in your photograph. (Have you had it blown up and framed yet?)

This habitual little mechanism is the naturally fearful part of you that has been developed to protect you from doing things that might invite change into your life. The voice may have been nurtured by you at a very early age, or when you were told repeatedly by someone in your life that you were no good. Generally it goes too far and has a knack of reminding you of every negative comment, insult, or self-criticism you have ever heard or made up. It's on a mission, and for some people this self-talk can ruin their lives, break their confidence, or sabotage their self-esteem. At the end of the day it's what goes on in your subconscious that shapes you—not the words that come out of your mouth.

These gremlins need to be tamed, quieted, or removed to allow you to move freely through your life. A little technique I use is to give the gremlin a squeaky, childish voice. Every time it tries to put me down or stop me from doing something, I've learned to laugh at it! You may decide that a different approach works better for you. Maybe you would like to gently quiet it down and ask it to go somewhere. If humor works for you, have a good laugh at it or with it. Giving it a voice, a name, or a face—maybe of someone you don't like—will make it more manageable. Try it the next time it stands in your way!

THE CONSCIOUS vs. THE SUBCONSCIOUS

Here lies a great challenge: When we express what we want in our lives and we say it with the greatest intentions in the world, if it is in conflict with our subconscious or deep-seated beliefs, then we won't be able to realize our ideal.

Rachel: Case Study

Rachel was one of my clients, and she wanted to become a counselor. She had inquired at the local college about a course and had enough money to do it, but she never quite got down to it. When I questioned Rachel about how she felt about doing the course and asked her to be really honest with me, these are the thoughts she was harboring in her subconscious that were stopping her from achieving her dreams:

"I often use the analogy of **life as a great big river.**"

- I haven't studied for years—what if I can't do it and don't pass the exams?
- What if I'm not bright enough to do the work?
- I probably wouldn't get a job after I got the qualifications anyway, so what's the point?
- I'd be scared in case I couldn't deal with the clients.
- I would be embarrassed to go to the classes— what if I had to read something out loud?

We are going to explore what your ideals are and then do a sifting process to find out exactly what thoughts or beliefs you are holding on to that are perhaps sabotaging your ideals, feelings, and emotions. Then I'll show you some powerful tools to change them. Keep reading! In Chapter 6 we'll explore what's lurking in your subconscious mind.

CREATIVE THINKING

Another powerful resource that we need to understand and implement to ensure that we achieve our aspirations and dreams is creative thinking. Creative thinking is essential if we want to add sparkle to our lives.

Most of us are in the habit of thinking in a more logical fashion rather than creatively. When we consider sharing a new business idea, or the idea of relocation to another country, how often do people remind us of everything that could go wrong? Any entrepreneur would tell us that to make a business a success, creative thinking is essential: Without imagination and creative problem-solving, businesses cannot survive. When we think back to the beginning of our relationships with our partners, we probably used our creativity to make an impression. Creative thinking is the lubricant that ensures that life flows easily and readily, and without it we can often feel stuck.

Like everything in life, creative thinking is a habit. As children we are resourceful and enjoy exercising our imagination. When we are small, we imagine how our lives are going to shape up, we imagine without the limitations of our minds, and believe that anything is possible. If we are fortunate, we develop the habit of creative thinking at home if not at school, but for most of us, creative thinking becomes a thing of the past, and as a result, we forget how to do it.

THE LITTLE BOY AND THE SNAIL

I watched a little boy of about six years old from a distance recently. He sat in his grandmother's garden with a pencil and paper, his hair was blond, and he had the most confident little face! He was gorgeous. He sat quietly while the other kids played, shouted, and screamed. He was drawing a picture of a snail, and he was so still.

This boy comes from a little mining village, and in a few years' time, the chances are he will forget about his passion for drawing and being still. Before he knows it he'll be 16. Where will he be then?

What creative things did you love to do as a child?

THE SCIENCE BEHIND THE BRAIN!

By measuring brain waves as individuals performed different tasks, neuroscientists have found that the two sides of the brain control very different activities.

LEFT BRAIN	RIGHT BRAIN
Words	Rhythm
Logic	Space
Numbers	Imagination
Sequence	Color
Linearity	Daydreaming
Analysis	Dimension
Lists	Holistic

In order to think creatively, human beings require the two sides of the brain to work together. Some people believe that they are more competent at right-brain activities and others the left, but the truth is that we are all capable of both. So many people say that they are not academic (left brain) or they are not artistic (right brain). Scientists have proven that we all have the capacity to be artistic or in some way academic, given the right training with the best teachers. This means that anyone's left- or right-brain thinking can be improved.

If someone goes to the gym three times a week and exercises just one side of their body, that side will become strong and firm. On the other hand, the side of their body that they don't exercise will become weak and limp. The truth is that to succeed or even to survive, creative thinking is absolutely necessary, which means we need to exercise both sides of the brain to become more creative.

Let's look here at how we can improve our creative thinking.

To be creative, we must feel relaxed, otherwise our physiology will do the job for us by breaking our concentration or creating stress-related illnesses to slow us down. When we relax, we have bursts of imagination and inspiration. Our problems can be solved . . .

- in a hot bath;
- on a lovely walk;
- when waking first thing in the morning;
- while dreaming, as our subconscious goes to work;
- listening to our favorite music;
  - out running or doing some sort of exercise;
    - while swimming;
    - when lying on a sandy beach; or
  - while doodling or playing.

What creative activities could you add to your life to exercise the right side of your brain? Here are some ideas, so why not try to implement two new ones into your life this week? Keep practicing this until you begin to do things that are breaking you out of your normal routine.

Cook something new
Mosaic a plant pot
Make some cushions
Gift-wrap something beautifully
Decorate a room
Restore a piece of furniture
Take some creative photographs
Arrange some unusual flowers
Set the table differently
Write someone a lovely letter
Send someone a beautiful message
Do something wildly romantic
Visit someone completely different
Go somewhere you haven't been before
Try some different food/wine

I often work with people who say they wouldn't know what to do if they had a day just for them. If this sounds like you, then over the years everyone else's needs have become more important than yours and you have never had to think of what you would really love to do with your time. Time passes by, kids grow up, we get divorced, we are laid off, we retire, and we find that we have so much time on our hands and often don't have a clue what to do with it. We stopped being creative years ago!

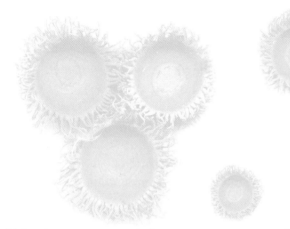

Whether you are in this situation or not, I would like to challenge you to make a day just for you. Make a list of all the things you would love to do. Be creative—list the wacky and the realistic, the practical and the indulgent. If at first it seems difficult, persevere. If you are really struggling, start with something for half an hour or an hour, and build it up each week.

If you begin to make excuses about how much things cost, take out the photo of yourself as a child and question what she/he deserves to be nurtured back to joy!

Choose from the following:

• Read a book in bed
• Take a long nap and spend the day pampering yourself
• Have a day out alone in a town you have never been to before
• Visit a museum or a historic site
   • Go for a picnic on the beach with your journal
      • Enjoy a spa day and luxuriate
      • Go to a ballet or to a symphony
      • Go to the movies
      • Go out to an exquisite restaurant
      • Have coffee at a coffeehouse or beautiful hotel
• Go to an art class
• Join a yoga class
• Race a sports car
• Fly a plane
• Take a scuba-diving lesson
• Visit an old school friend
• Go for salsa lessons
• Take guitar lessons
• Go to a cooking class
• Visit an animal shelter

FLOW . . . "NATURAL PROZAC"

When creativity is flowing, when we are truly happy and our left and right brains are in perfect harmony, we are in a state of flow. Have you ever started something and before you knew it the day has flown by and you hadn't realized the time? Have you ever worked on a project and just loved every minute? I often hear people speak of when they were "in flow." This is the place that creativity is made. When the right and the left brain connect, the state called "flow" arises. We have all the logical and analytical skill, expertise, and information to support our artistic and intuitive ideas. We are off . . . and the situation we are in just works!

When we are in flow, it's the greatest feeling in the world, and often we can be in flow with projects at work when we have the necessary skill. We often find ourselves in flow when we have the right chemistry and compatibilities in a relationship. We love the feeling when we are eating the right food and the diet is working. All of these states create "feel-good feelings," which in turn release our internal chemistry to make us feel on top of the world.

When we do what we love, we feel wonderful, and the impact on repairing and restoring our mind, body, and spirit is greater than we could ever imagine.

Remember a time when you were in love. When we fall in love, it's almost as if we could take on the world single-handed. When we fall head over heels, we feel optimistic and upbeat, leaving others puzzled as they wonder why we look so different. When we fall in love, a whole range of chemicals rush through our bodies making us feel absolutely fantastic. Our immune systems are boosted . . . very rarely do people who fall in love have bad colds or sore throats! It's a fantastic physiological frenzy that is taking place inside our bodies. This experience can clear up depression, heal tumors, and cure illnesses— and it's all activated by us.

I'm not suggesting for a moment that you go out and fall in love with someone new. The same physiological response can be activated if you fall in love with *life*. When we become passionate about our life, the same type of responses can occur. It's the most powerful healer, and it's at our fingertips.

THE REPTILIAN BRAIN STATE . . . WHEN WE ARE STRESSED OUT

It's a fact of life that for every positive there is a negative. The opposite of the flow state is called the "reptilian brain state," where the left and the right brain are not connecting. Perhaps we are full of great ideas, but we just can't get them off the ground, as we don't have the logic or the skill to support or implement them. Or, alternately, we are overloaded with practical skills, but we don't have the creative capacity or insight to achieve our dreams.

In the reptilian brain state, we often feel stuck, stressed, or frustrated about our current situation. We might feel trapped, with no choices. We cannot see our way forward in life, and this is the most difficult place in the world to be. In the reptilian brain state, we cannot come up with solutions; we don't have the knowledge or experience to get out of the situation. We can often feel depressed, apathetic, bored, frustrated, anxious, and unhappy.

Unlike flow, where our internal pharmacy releases a rush of feel-good chemicals, in this state we can often find ourselves suffering from illnesses and ailments that the body is producing to remind us that something needs to change! How often are we handed drugs as a temporary measure for situations that need attention in our lives? If our blood pressure goes up, do we question how we are dealing with life, or do we expect the medicine to sort out the problem? I know there are times when conventional medicine is essential and can be helpful, but so much is symptomatic of the situations in our lives at that time.

I was in the reptilian brain state for almost a year. I regularly went to my local doctor for a host of little ailments. I'd gone from being an extremely confident and sociable person to someone who didn't want to go out. I didn't want guests, I felt insecure, and for the first time in my life, I felt no passion for the future. I couldn't see past today and couldn't understand what was happening.

I didn't really tell anyone how I was feeling because I thought I'd risk showing weakness and that I might be perceived as failing to be the perfect mother. For the first time in my life, I was helpless about virtually everything.

The bottom line was that I wanted to work *and* look after Liberty. I wanted to express my creativity as well as being a mom. Even if I'd had a part-time job, I would have been happy; however, my little gremlin and my

belief structure were strangling me. After a year I took some well-deserved time out to talk with like-minded people and began to explore and find creative solutions to improve my life. In the reptilian brain state, we need to take some time away from the situation and work out what we need to do. We need to analyze our thoughts and make sure that we are thinking rationally. To do this we need to take some time out just for *us* to consider exactly what we would love to do to make life a bit more fun.

IS YOUR FEAR FACT OR FICTION?

Did you know that 90 percent of our fears are just illusions or *what-if* scenarios? When we actually analyze our fears, we often find out that they are:

False
Expectations
Appearing
Real!

Yet many of us spend much of our time dwelling on what might happen in a negative way rather than focusing on the really positive outcomes that we could achieve. Can you imagine how different your life would feel if only you could change this habit? Worrying is just another habit that you get into, and I do appreciate that it's much easier said than done to actually give it up, but if you analyze the things you worry about and work out how you would deal with the consequences if they really were to happen, you could save yourself a whole lot of time and heartache. If you begin to retrain your brain to remind yourself that no matter what happens you will be able to deal with it because you've dealt with so much before, you could be well on your way to stopping the worrying battle.

Realistically, almost all the things you worry about will probably never happen. Again, the job here is learning to tame the gremlins!

GMTV WITH LORRAINE KELLY

About four years ago I decided that to take these coping strategies out to as many people as possible, I was going to have to target TV. My target audience was the *LK Today* morning show with UK presenter Lorraine Kelly. After one or two phone calls to GMTV, I met with the producers of the program. I was so encouraged by the meeting, as they felt they could use me and they were going to look at where they could fit me into the show. I was so pleased that I bought myself a bottle of Laurent Perrier pink champagne . . . I love the gorgeous floral tin it comes in! This was my treat for myself for doing so well in the meeting.

PANIC ATTACKS

When I got back to Edinburgh, I was optimistic, but not naive enough to believe that just because I got a positive response in the meeting, I would actually get the spot on the show. One day later, to my absolute amazement, GMTV rang: They wanted to check my schedule! I couldn't believe my luck. Then something very interesting happened.

Once I hung up the phone, my heart started thumping, and my mind started racing. My palms were sweating, and for the first time in my life, I was having a panic attack. I raced over to a friend's place who had been involved in lots of television and I told him what had just happened. He said he was delighted for me and thought I'd be brilliant. Then I started to question myself. I said that I didn't think I could do it. He was baffled and laughed. He said, "You're a confidence coach, of course you can do it!" I couldn't get through to him, and he couldn't understand that I just couldn't do it. I was terrified. I had just realized one of my dreams, and now I simply couldn't go through with it.

I then went down to my Aunt Margaret's and told her the news. She asked, "What is it that you are frightened of?" I said, "I don't know. I just know that I can't do it." Then I said to myself: *What is little Dawn frightened of, the Dawn in the photo . . .* At that point I asked for a pen and some paper, and one by one I began to write down and analyze my fears. This is what came up . . .

- I'm not attractive enough
- I'm not intelligent enough
- I'm too rough around the edges
- I don't have a degree in psychology
- What if I make a fool of myself?

These were all my old, negative beliefs that I thought were dead and buried; however, in my moment of success they had decided to ambush me! One by one I rationalized and reframed each of them, and before I knew it, the panic began to settle.

- *I'm not attractive* turned into *Of course you are.*
- *I'm not intelligent* became *Yes, I am, not in an academic way, but I sure am bright.*
- *I am too rough around the edges for television . . .* well, that disappeared years ago, and I'm

very proud that I come from a little mining village.

- *I don't have a degree in psychology,* but I have the life experience to understand people, and I've been teaching myself for about five years!

Then my Aunt Margaret asked me, "What else are you frightened of? Why do you think you will make a fool of yourself?" I then came out with the golden nugget! I was frightened that the camera would come up to my face and knock me off my track while I was talking to Lorraine. I was imagining how Lorraine would be embarrassed and not know where to look, then I would panic and probably start crying because I'd blown my biggest opportunity in television. My Aunt Margaret smiled and said to me, "Dawn, this is the 21st century. Cameras have zoom lenses, darling." We laughed! As it happened, when I appeared on the program I wasn't nervous at all; however, my worst nightmare actually did happen and I lost my train of thought. It's as if I had to test myself! I recovered in a split second, and no one at home would have noticed.

How often are your fears and worries just false expectations appearing real? I didn't even know that these fears and limiting beliefs existed in my subconscious. Often we bury them so deeply that we don't even know they are there. So often when we feel the physical symptoms of fear, we don't explore the possibilities of our dreams—we just give up. The next time you feel the symptoms, write down as many reasons as you can why you are afraid, and then challenge and reframe the beliefs.

Make a list of your fears and work through them as I did in the exercise above. If you really want to challenge yourself, work this through with a friend who supports you and wants the best for you. If you don't have someone, use the mentor in your mind!

"Many of us spend much of our time dwelling on what **might happen.**"

WHAT SHAPED YOU?

In the previous chapter, we looked at how we have developed habits, beliefs, and thoughts from a whole range of different influences in our lives.

The media bombards us with mixed messages. Images of beautiful, slim women in skimpy clothes, for example, often leave us with feelings of lack and self-hatred, yet at the same time we have a thirst to be that shape. So many of our beliefs are created by external influences.

Which of the following have had a great influence on you, on the way you think and behave in your life? Identify your three greatest influences, and list in what way they have affected how you think about yourself today.

Church	Society
Culture	Friends
Family	Peers
Bosses	Employees
Siblings	TV
Reading	Groups
Newspapers	Partners
Parents	Children

There is a very high possibility that your parents will be in your top three. Our parents influence us from the second we are born. Try this exercise.

STOP

Even if your parents were really critical, judgmental, angry, harsh, or impatient, and you don't feel at all like them, be aware of how you treat yourself. What is your internal self-talk? What are your gremlins? You may have changed your external habits, but the internal characteristics may still lurk!

Whatever your findings, this is not an opportunity to blame your parents for doing what they have done to you. There would be absolutely no point in that! However, we do need to recognize that they were only doing the best they could with the knowledge they had at the time. Your parents were probably blissfully unaware of what they were doing; they probably inherited traits and characteristics from their parents, who, in turn, were only doing the best they could.

So now, as the parent of your children, you must be aware that you influence them hugely, and until you begin to change, they are

going to inherit all of your good and bad habits! Some people ask me if it's too late to change now that their kids have grown up. I always say that it's never too late to talk to your children. At the same time, it's important to be aware that some children are very resistant to parents' influences. I'm sure we all know of angry, manipulative, cynical, negative, difficult, and very insecure children, and no matter how good the parent is, no amount of positive parenting can change their behavior. All we can do is our very best, and know when to draw the line and accept them for the way they are—otherwise, we will have a difficult and very challenging life. When parents behave in a particular way or have a certain viewpoint, it will have an impact on their children—they will either accept it or reject it, but it will have an impact of some kind. I remember reading an article in the press about Prince Charles's father, who made a very negative public comment about his son. I remember in a BBC Radio interview being asked if I thought it would have any effect on him. My response was that of course it would. No matter how old we are, our parents' opinions count, whether we show it or not! It's almost as if the child inside is always vulnerable, whether we are 5 or 50 or 80 years old.

On the lines below, list all the strengths and the weaknesses of the person or people who brought you up. Who were your biggest influences? List them. Think of how they treated you as you were growing up.

Name...
[Don't fill your name in until the end of this exercise]

Strengths   **Weaknesses**

....
....
....
....
....
....
....
....

Choose from headings such as:

Judgmental	Supportive	Critical	Encouraging
Alcoholic	Fun	Depressed	Well balanced
Negative	Optimistic	Arrogant	Caring
Cynical	Sensitive	Perfectionist	Laid-back
Blunt	Gentle	Unsupportive	Risk taker
Oversensitive	Adventurous	Overbearing	Easygoing
Poor listener	Good listener	Always right	Good communicator
Stubborn	Flexible	Rude	Polite
Volatile	Happy	Angry	Honest
Aggressive	Trustworthy	Dishonest	Bright
Chauvinistic	Open	Too liberal	Overpowering
Sexist	Manipulative	Closed	

Anything else you can think of?

Now put your name at the top. Yes, I've tricked you, but give this a try! Now, circle all the traits that are yours. Take your time and really think about this.

What did you find? Chances are that you are identifying your mother or father's traits—or you may have changed everything about yourself to be as different as you can from your parents.

Recently I was asked to do some television work in London. Although in my heart and soul I really wanted to take these opportunities, it meant moving to England with my daughter. My mom had been widowed 18 months previously, and I was concerned about my daughter moving schools. I was also apprehensive that Mom, who had never moved to another town, would say, "Don't do it; it will cause too much disruption in your life." I was flabbergasted one evening when she said to me, "You have to go for this, Dawn. If it means moving, you've got to do it!" I was so excited. I had her blessing, and she was happy for me. If the situation had been reversed, I would have had a long, hard emotional struggle on my hands. Letting me go was the best thing she could have done for me. When parents impress their fears on us, they prevent us from following our dreams.

CHAPTER SIX

How Would You Love Your Life to Be?

Hopefully the last chapter highlighted a good chunk of the many familiar blocks that you may stumble across each time you consider making any kind of significant change in your life. We're now going to test the process and see what else is lurking. We are making progress . . . however, we still have a long way to go! In the following exercises, imagine you have just entered the world of Alice in Wonderland! You have opened the door and spread out in front of you, in glorious technicolor, is a life that you would really love to live—a life that is loving, happy, and filled with contentment and joy.

know this might sound a bit strange and very uncomfortable to do, and your gremlins will probably be trying to burst out of their cage to tell you not to be silly, as life could never be this way for *you!* Come with me on this one—really work hard. I need you to suspend all your limiting and negative thoughts and shut out your gremlins! Once you have done this, allow your right brain to kick in and be really creative. In your imagination, you can do anything you want to do, go anywhere you want to go, and have any feelings you want to have. What would that life look like for you?

EXERCISE 1
List five things that would make the picture of your ideal life really complete for you.

1.

2.

3.

4.

5.

Think about how it would be to:

Feel confident	Relax more	Leave your partner	Speak to someone you like
Go back to college	Take some night classes	Be well again	Lose weight
Stop smoking	Change jobs	Set up your own business	Let your struggle go
Forgive someone	Stop feeling guilty	Let go of the past	Stop being angry
Vacation in Canada	Visit family abroad	Move abroad	Have a home by the sea
Have a nice car	Buy a computer	Buy a house	Move home
Pay off your debt	Make new friends	Express how you feel	Meet someone special
Have time for you	Speak your mind	Vacation in Thailand	Go on a safari in Africa

EXERCISE 2

Once you have done this, list all the benefits that you, your family, and everyone in your life would experience as a result of your life being this way. Think of the emotional benefits, the financial benefits, and the impact on you and everyone around you. List the benefits for each of the different ideals.

1.

2.

3.

4.

5.

Happier	More energetic
More money	More security for the future
More fulfilled	Inner peace
Less stressed	People would like me more
More relaxed	More time for everyone else
Life would feel easier	Feel free
Daily struggle would end	Impact on my health
Less nervous	Well-being would improve
More confident	More joy

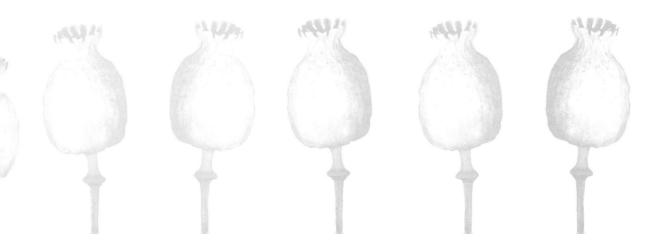

EXERCISE 3

List all the reasons why you aren't living these ideals at the moment. Write down every reason why you can't have this ideal in your life—the tangible reasons, financial reasons, emotional reasons, fears, feelings of lack—everything that stops you from having each of them. The more you write down here, and the more effort you put into this exercise, the better the result will be. GO FOR IT!

1.

2.

3.

4.

5.

Once again you can see in black and white the beliefs and thoughts that you live with. These beliefs are keeping the doors to your future dreams and aspirations firmly closed!

Now, I'd like you to go back up to the top of the list and begin to circle everything that is just an *excuse*. Imagine that you are supporting your best friend and he or she has asked you to help him or her reach their ideals. Really question whether the things you have written are realistic or if they are just beliefs that you have developed that stop you from even considering your ideal life!

Now read this list again, and let's see if you can recognize any of your beliefs. Once you have read through these, try to cross out any more excuses from your list.

NO TIME

Do you feel that you never have enough time to do what you would really love to do? Is time always against you? Is your calendar packed with commitments for the kids or for work? Get planning! You really need to sit down and look at your timetable for the coming days and weeks, and begin a new planning strategy.

If you really want to make something happen in your life, then you need to plan—fail to plan and plan to fail! If you don't make the time, nothing will change. Really question your beliefs that revolve around time—is it just a matter of planning? On a scale of one to ten, how much do you want this ideal? If it's around ten, then make the time; if it's less than ten, do you really want it? If it's less than ten, what's stopping it from being a ten?

STOP!

Be aware of time not really being the issue. Is the real issue the fact that you never feel deserving of putting yourself first? Are your needs always less important than everyone else's?

Case Study

In one of my workshops, Emily asked me how she could make her life feel like less of a routine. She had a successful but stressful career in human resources; she also had two children who had busy social lives. She looked after the house, the kids, and her husband—who also had a busy career. When we looked at the plan of her life, it was absolutely crazy! Something in her life was going to have to change. She needed to drop out of some of the commitments for the kids, work part-time, or get help around the house. In her current position she couldn't work part-time, so that wasn't an option. She wasn't prepared to cut down on the kids' commit-

ments, so the only real option was for her to have housekeeping help. Emily managed to come up with every excuse under the sun for not having a cleaning service. When we analyzed it further, we realized that her belief was that she would see herself as lazy if she brought in help. She couldn't imagine paying someone to do something that she saw as her responsibility . . . but if she didn't get some help, her life would continue to be so stressful that she would one day become ill because she just couldn't manage the load.

NO MONEY

Do you feel that you just don't have the cash to do what you want to do? Do you feel that you give up on your dreams before you even begin because the idea of never having enough money always blocks you? Get creative!

Brutal truth time again! Even people who have money at one time may have not at another time. If you don't have the money, how can you find another way to achieve the goal? Imagine you are trying to help someone else achieve their dream. How could you encourage them? Where there is a will there is a way . . . if you aren't too creative, ask someone to help you work out a way.

On a scale of one to ten, how much do you want this

ideal? If it's near a ten, then it's worth the hard work and effort to go for it! If you just can't:

STOP!

Be aware of the real issue here—are you too lazy to make the effort to achieve your goal? Is the real issue motivation?

Case Study

In so many of my workshops people say they would love to go on a vacation of a lifetime to Africa, Canada, Thailand, or India. Time after time, the same old excuse comes up: "We don't have the money." If you want something enough, then sometimes it's worth waiting for. If you really want it, why not plan to go there in 18 months' time? Start to watch out for special offers and deals—once you are tuned in to the idea, opportunities begin to appear. Again, this is about getting creative. If you want it to happen, *make it happen!*

COMMUNICATION

Do you feel you would love to do so many things in your life, but other people always stop you from going for your goals and dreams? Do you constantly think that if you even bothered to share what you want to do, it would fall on deaf ears and would be a wasted effort anyway? Share your ideas!

If you don't express how important something is to you, then no one will ever know. Your ideal will remain a secret to everyone but you. Or one day you will feel you have had enough and will do whatever your heart desires regardless of anyone else and regardless of the consequences. Neither of these scenarios are favorable—communication is imperative!

On a scale of one to ten, how much do you want the ideal that is being blocked by a communication problem? If it's a ten, get talking!

STOP!

Be aware that the real issue could have to do with self-esteem or assertiveness rather than an actual communication problem. Often we are too frightened to communicate how we feel. Don't worry if low self-esteem is the issue—we'll get to this very soon.

Case Study

I remember a girl who said she had always wanted to go to college but couldn't afford to give up work. I knew the large insurance company she worked for. They were very proactive in staff development, and I asked her if the company would pay for her tuition while she continued to work. She didn't think that her boss would agree so she had never considered the possibility. When she was setting her goals, she decided she was going to ask her boss. I received a thank-you card the next week. He said YES!

LOW SELF-ESTEEM

Do you feel that you aren't deserving of things? Do you ever feel like a victim or a doormat? Are you frightened to say no, in case you upset people's feelings—yet your own feelings are never taken into account? Do you feel that people walk over you all the time?

"Do you feel you would love to do so many things in your life, but other people always stop you from going for your goals and dreams?"

SPEAK UP FOR YOURSELF

If this sounds like you, then you may be suffering from low self-esteem or a lack of self-confidence. What we will do here is help you build boundaries and teach you how to stick to them. We also need to teach you to say no and stand up for what you want and need. Once we do that, you will feel a boost in your self-esteem and you will notice that other people's reactions begin to change toward you . . . life will begin to feel different.

Without boundaries in our lives, we feel victimized and miss out on opportunities, as we are not able to stand up for what we truly believe. (See Part II of this book.)

Case Study

A lady I worked with had a great personality, was married with three kids, and had a busy full-time job. Somehow everyone else's needs had become more important than her own. She held great resentment toward her husband, and I feared that the only way she could see herself moving forward was to ditch him! I suggested that she shouldn't be too hasty. Many people feel the need to blame someone else, when really the problem has to do with their lack of assertiveness—not making time for themselves or doing the things they really want to do.

She began to introduce time into her life for herself, and did little things for herself—she'd take long baths, go swimming, and ask her husband to pick up the kids, and in three weeks' time she felt much better. After 15 years, her relationship began to blossom. Her husband had become happier, as she was less insecure and became interested in herself and her own life, which took the focus off his.

AGE

How often have you thought that you are too old? Too old for what? I often hear people say that age is the main reason they aren't doing what they would love to do. You are only as young or old as you tell yourself. You can vastly improve your life if you just take the focus off the date of your birth. Experience comes with age, wisdom comes with age, and knowledge comes with age, and they are all to be celebrated. These are the things that really count in your life, but if you continue to see your age negatively, then you will wrinkle away into your old age and block all your future happiness. Age is only a number. Isn't that what you would tell your friends?

Case Study

I worked with a lady who had dreamed of becoming a schoolteacher. When we were looking at what she wanted to do for a career change, she said that she would love to go to college and retrain; however, her only block was that she was 35 years old and she felt she was too old to study. When I asked her to rationalize her statement, she got stuck.

FEAR

Are you always worrying? Do you play pictures over and over in your mind of all the things that could go wrong if you actually made changes in your life? Do you imagine the worst possible outcome in most situations? It's 90 percent illusion.

If this sounds familiar to you, then chances are that you are pretty frightened of playing with life. Fearful and worrying thoughts are bad habits that we acquire along the way in our lives. Research has proven that 90 percent of our fears and things that we actually worry about never ever happen!

In the previous chapter, we looked at how we can analyze our fears and worries, and how to quiet the gremlins and begin to relax with life. If we don't address our fears and our worries, we can become stuck, feeling terrorized and afraid. If we harness these habits, we can begin to truly enhance our lives.

Case Study

One of my clients wanted to leave her abusive relationship. When she thought about the consequences of doing so, she often felt physically sick. Although she was abused constantly, she worried that her partner might harm himself if she left. She imagined that his family—whom she didn't particularly like anyway—would never speak to her again. She imagined that her partner would steal her children—though legally she would be protected. She imagined that she wouldn't be able to manage on her own—even though within the relationship, she was living by herself anyway. The fear paralyzed her until she began to work through the process of analyzing each and every single fear, and she realized that, for herself and for the children, she needed to do this . . . AND SOON!

CHAPTER SEVEN

The Power of Positive Affirmations

How to shape our thought patterns to influence our lives for the better.

This is the most important section in the book. If you manage to "get this," you will be well on your way to creating the kind of life you really want to live. We are going to look at the amazing impact that your thoughts have on your physiology. The practical exercises will demonstrate how your thoughts have power over how you feel. We will look at how our thoughts determine our motivation levels, influence our health, impact our well-being, create our confidence, and affect every emotion that we have— every single day of our lives.

Just before we begin, I'd like you to try these two practical exercises to show you how feeding your mind can activate your internal physiology to give you whatever response you need.

THE LEMON EXERCISE

1. Ask someone to read you this passage or read it to yourself and imagine every detail.
2. If you don't like lemons, replace the word *lemon* with another citrus fruit—say, a lime or grapefruit.
3. Sit comfortably and close your eyes.

Imagine that you are in the Australian outback. Picture yourself with a sandy desert all around you. The sand is brick-red in color, it's red hot under your feet, and it stretches for miles and miles. Imagine looking up at the gorgeous blue cloudless sky that stretches all around, empty except for the blazing yellow sun rising in the sky. You are in this desert alone, you feel safe and secure, and you are curious about what is around you. As the sun rises, you begin to feel hotter and hotter. The perspiration is pouring down your chest and back and you begin to feel a little dehydrated.

Imagine now that your mouth is becoming very dry and all you can think of is water. As you breathe in, you feel your nostril hairs begin to scorch. It's now becoming unbearably hot. Imagine the feeling of the sun penetrating through your skin and into your bones.

Imagine that your mouth is feeling completely dry and your lips feel like they are cracking in the midday sun. You feel really uncomfortable, and all you can think about is finding some cool, fresh drinking water. You see nothing for miles so you begin to run, and as you do, you become even hotter and thirstier.

Suddenly, out of nowhere, standing in front of you is a tall, gray rock face. The rock face reaches up to the sky, and as you run toward it, you are instantly shaded from the burning hot sun. The shade cools your skin.

You begin to run around the rock face in the hopes that you will find an entrance. Your mouth is bone dry. Then you find an opening; slowly you make your way in, hoping to find some cool, fresh drinking water. Imagine the feeling as you move into the cavern: Gentle shafts of light stream in through an opening in the ceiling and you hear the drip, drip, dripping sound of running water. You begin to look for the water. Your feet are scorched, and all you want is to quench your thirst.

Imagine that you come across a tree bearing large, juicy, ripe, yellow lemons. Just imagine that to quench your thirst you take the waxy fruit in your hand, holding it up to your nose and smelling the fresh fruit. Then in an absolute frenzy to quench your thirst, you take the fruit into your hands—think of that amazing smell—and tear it open. Imagine as you do, a squirt of the refreshing, zesty juice hits your lips and mouth. Remember that amazing fresh flavor. In an instant, the taste radiates throughout your body, then you bite into the juicy fruit. The taste is deliciously refreshing. Your mouth is filled with saliva, and in an instant, your thirst is totally quenched.

Your Response

1. Did you imagine the taste of the lemon/fruit in your mouth?
2. Was there saliva in your mouth at the end of the exercise?
3. At some point in the exercise, did you imagine that your mouth was dry?

Most people have some sort of physical response. Some salivate at the thought of biting into the lemon or citrus fruit. Others feel that their mouth is dry when they imagine walking in the hot sun, and in their imagination they taste the lemon.

The brain, or our imagination, will respond to whatever we tell it. It cannot differentiate between what is true or false. The brain will always create a response to whatever we feed it. In this instance, we told the brain that it was tasting a lemon, so the brain responded by creating the necessary responses throughout our physiological system to activate our internal pharmacy and drive the mechanism that creates saliva in our mouths.

Let's imagine that each day we tell our brain we are feeling low, depressed, frightened, or sad. Can you imagine the physiological response these thoughts have on your emotions and feelings? Many of us aren't even aware of what we are thinking. It's important that we analyze our thoughts on a conscious and subconscious level and correct these thoughts to ensure that we feel okay every day.

This exercise was a revelation for me. For the first time, I could see how my mind could control my emotions. I realized that I could control my energy levels, my well-being, my health, and my confidence. The way I felt was actually being driven by the thoughts I was thinking about myself and my life each day.

EXERCISE

TURN YOUR HEAD 360 degrees!
In this exercise, I'd like you to:

1. Ask someone to read the following instructions to you.
2. Stand about three feet in front of a wall.
3. Face away from the wall.
4. Stand very still—don't move any part of your body from your shoulders to your toes.
5. Move your head and neck in Steps 1 and 3 ONLY. (If you have chronic neck pain, be gentle with yourself, but do try—you might be surprised at the results!)

STEP 1

With your eyes open, stand with your feet slightly apart. Keep your shoulders relaxed and facing the front. Keep your feet to the front. Cross your arms underneath your chest. Keep your whole body from the neck down to your toes perfectly still.

When you are ready, turn your head over your right shoulder as far as you possibly can, and in your mind, mark a point on the wall. Then slowly turn your head back to the front . . . and relax.

STEP 2

This time, close your eyes and do the exercise in your imagination only. Make sure you don't move your head during this part of the exercise. Imagine that you have some rubber in your neck and this means you can turn your neck and head very easily. Imagine that you are turning your head back to the point that you marked on the wall. Once you have reached the point on the wall in your imagination, imagine that you are now turning your head 180 degrees, right around to the back of the room. Feel the strain as you turn.

Once you have done that, imagine that you are turning it all the way around in a full circle. Feel the strain. Imagine turning your head around in a full circle, 360 degrees. Then come gently back to the front . . . and relax. Keep your eyes closed, and when you are ready, try this again.

In your imagination, go back to the marked point on the wall, but this time go beyond it. Go farther, all the way to the back of the room. Turn your head 180 degrees; feel the strain. Then move all the way around in a full circle once again—360 degrees, all the way back to the front, and relax.

STEP 3

This time repeat Step 1. With your eyes open, turn your head over your right shoulder, going as far as you possibly can. In your mind, mark a new point on the wall. Once you have done that, bring your head back to the front and relax.

What did you find?

Did you find that you turned farther on the second attempt?
Why do you think your head turned farther the second time?

By visualizing turning your head around farther, your brain activated your internal physiological mechanisms to prepare you for the expected outcome. In this instance, the brain sent a chemical response to relax the muscles in your neck so that you could turn it farther!

THE ZONE

Imagine a newly qualified Olympic athlete as he stands at the starting line. This is his first time in the Olympics. The stadium is bursting at the seams, the crowds are cheering, the television cameras are firmly focused and totally unfor-giving. In a split second, the young athlete is overwhelmed and loses his focus. Imagine how he feels as he looks around and his stomach begins to churn. He begins to look nervously at the other runners. He thinks: *These are the big boys and I don't stand a chance here.*

When the starter's pistol fires, his confidence and focus have gone . . . and because of this, so has his opportunity!

Olympic athletes often reach the track and run faster than they have ever run in their lives before. They are oblivious of the crowds, the cameras, and the competitors around them. They are focused internally, in control of the internal as well as the external game. They enter a place called "the zone," where they hear and see absolutely nothing around them. Their mind is so firmly focused on the finishing line and the fact that they are going to run faster than they have ever run before that when the starter's pistol fires, they head off like a bullet, believing they will run faster than they have ever done in their lives. And on many occasions, that is exactly what they do, reaching records that they never imagined they could achieve.

When we focus strongly and gear ourselves up to be physically better than we have ever been before, we alert the internal pharmacy to produce outstanding physical results. This exercise can be applied to mental agility: When we focus on our goal or desired outcome and refuse to allow anyone or anything to stand in the way, then we begin to achieve the kind of life we want to live.

WHAT IS AN AFFIRMATION?

Affirmations are statements that we repeat over and over in our minds to create various outcomes and emotions in our lives. Many people do affirmations without even knowing it! Have you ever done any of the following?

• Gone for a job and thought to yourself—*I am going to get this job, no matter what.* And with all the will in the world, you went for the job, and got it!
• Met someone and thought to yourself, *I am going to date you. I want you.* And by believing so hard and doing everything you can, you began to date that person.
• Believed something with all your will and thought the thought over and over without any question until you believed it so much that you made it happen?

If you have, you have practiced the art of POSITIVE AFFIRMATIONS, and it's highly probable that you have had at least one positive outcome. Positive affirmations are quite simply very positive statements that are set clearly in the direction of the goal or emotion that you want to realize. The opposite is a negative affirmation. This is a statement that you may:

• not be aware of if it is stored in your subconscious;
• be repeating over and over in your mind; or
• reveal in conversation from time to time.

One thing is for sure—these statements of belief will stall or even stop you from achieving your desired goals or outcomes. They could be determining so many of your habits you aren't even aware of, so you need to be extra diligent to ensure that you don't have any unwanted, dysfunctional statements that are sabotaging your future whizzing around in your head!

Here are some examples of NEGATIVE AFFIRMATIONS. Has this ever happened to you? Have you ever thought the following?

• *I'll never get that job, I'm not bright enough* —you go for the interview, and don't get the job.
• *He or she would never want to go out with me, I'm not attractive enough*—you do nothing, say nothing, and nothing ever evolves with the person you admire.
• *Nothing good ever happens to me in my life* —and it doesn't.

All of these negative statements have an impact on what you do in your life, and they ultimately stop you from achieving joy. Try this . . . listen to conversations with friends.

1. Listen to friends who are happy. What are they saying about themselves and their lives? What positive affirmations do they reveal in conversation? Positive, optimistic people speak positively and optimistically. They constantly make positive statements about themselves and the world.

2. Listen to people who are stuck and somehow never get out of the rut. Listen to their language . . . what do they believe about themselves, and what is their view of life? Many of these people are caught up in negative thinking and can't get out of it. Often they have negative ingrained beliefs and to back them up they feed their minds with as much misery and disaster as they can.

To ensure that we live life to the fullest, we must become aware of what we are feeding our minds. If we are feeding our minds negative affirmations, then our outcomes are going to be negative and destructive and we will continue to feel low and frustrated with life. If, on the other hand, we feed our minds with positive affirmations, then our outcomes are going to become more positive and constructive. In the following pages, we are going to look at how we can begin to build a really strong supportive and proactive dialogue for you to use in your everyday life. This will enhance your relationships, self-confidence, health and well-being, working life, relaxation, and creative time!

WHAT ARE YOU FEEDING YOUR MIND?

Every day our brains are bombarded with messages. Depending on what our habits are, each of these messages will be forming our

"Bad news sells and good news is never really promoted."

perceptions of the world. Each of the following has a huge impact on the way we see things.

THE BAD NEWS

How often do you read the newspapers or watch the news on TV? Have you noticed that bad news sells and good news is never really promoted?! Are you addicted to following a murder investigation? Do you feel fearful of life because of what you read in the press? Do you read about horrendous events and imagine that they might happen to you or your family? Do you spend time discussing the detail of these negative news stories with your friends and family?

If you do, then you are constantly affirming to yourself how terrible the world is. You are developing a belief that will influence your emotions and your every move. I'm not saying that you shouldn't be aware of what is going on in the world. We must ensure that we are safe and protected, but focusing on bad news will affect the way we think and feel from day to day. I think it's a bit bizarre that we like to hear about death, disaster, murder, and misery rather than listen to joyful and happy stories.

READING POPULAR MAGAZINES

How do you feel about your body image? Do you compare the way you look with the faces and bodies of the airbrushed models in popular magazines? I can remember doing some market research for a Web-development project. The research had to do with the difference between male and female preferences. With the exception of *Here's Health* magazine, I don't subscribe to any magazines, so I began my research from scratch. My first idea was to buy 20 "female" magazines and 20 "male" magazines. At the end of two weeks, I realized that I was feeling self-conscious about my shape and the way that I looked. I had been reading these magazines from cover to cover, and as I did, my eyes were taking in images of slinky, stunningly beautiful women. I realized that subconsciously I had been comparing myself to them. I felt overweight and unattractive and had to begin yet another regime of positive body and face affirmations! Be aware of your little internal gremlins as you flick through the pages of your next "feel-good" magazine!

BEST FRIENDS

Whoever we surround ourselves with in our lives will influence the way we think. If we have happy, optimistic, successful friends and family, they will have a positive impact on us. My friends Mhairi and Lynda are good examples.

Lynda works in the oil industry in the U.S. She's sporty, competitive, and it would appear that whatever she puts her mind to, she achieves. When I have a challenge, I talk it through with her. She has a practical, eternally optimistic viewpoint and always encourages me to do the very best I can. She is confident and self-assured, which enables me to be confident and self-assured in her company. I always feel refreshed after having a good chat with her.

Mhairi is entrepreneurial, a risk-taker, creative, and sensual. In her company I relax, and we talk in an encouraging and gentle way. By supporting one another, no challenge is too great to take on.

Spending time with friends like these is a bit like taking the most potent vitamin tablet in the world.

On the other hand, I have had one or two friends who always see the negative in any situation. Sometimes they come and tell me about their problems, which they never seem to do anything about. They remind me of all the bad things that are going on in their lives and in the world, and when they leave the house, I feel flat and low in energy.

What impact are the people around you having on the way you feel each day?

A POSITIVE INFLUENCE

I made it my mission seven years ago to begin to read lots of positive, upbeat books. I loved reading case studies of people who had made real life changes. At that time I was employed in an advertising sales role. My company car was like a little personal-development library. I'd travel one hour each day from Edinburgh to Glasgow, and in my car I would listen and learn. I felt so positively charged as the personal-development tapes shaped my new mind-set, and the impact on my sales figures was astounding.

If you get something out of this book, why not build a routine into your life to create some personal time to refocus and feed your mind exactly what it needs? Consider some of the following and how much time or influence they are having in your life.

What's influencing your belief processes right now? Are any of the following bad habits creating your perception of life?

• Reading daily newspapers for the bad news
• Watching TV for the bad news
• Watching trashy talk shows
• Watching violent movies
• Watching soaps every day
• Reading popular magazines
• Gossiping with friends/family
• Sharing negative news with friends/family

Each of these habits reinforces negative affirmations about the world we live in. If they dominate your intake of information, there is probably no space in your mind for joy, inspiration, hope, and a sense of belief in some greater power at work in your life.

You may have read the above list and felt that all the joy would be taken out of your life if you were to give up all these bad habits. For some people, if they were to give them up their world would be empty.

Try this exercise to test how much you are addicted to each of the above bad habits.

EXERCISE

1. Rank your habits on a scale of 1–10. 1 = you love doing this activity, 10 = you could easily give it up.

2. Choose at least one habit that you could consider giving up for the next two weeks.

3. Do this process gradually until you eliminate the negative focus from your daily life.

If you feel that your life would be empty if you were to give up your bad habits, the following ideas may offer you some options for building positive affirmations about the world into your daily life. Each one might reinforce a sense of joy, inspiration, hope, and belief.

- Read personal development books
- Pray
- Write down ten reasons to be grateful each day
- Read inspirational biographies
- Take up creative hobbies
- Begin to play a musical instrument
- Watch the *Discovery Channel*
- Watch some inspirational movies
- Read health and fitness magazines
- Share good news stories with people
- Limit your intake of bad news each day
- Only speak positively about people

This week try to integrate some positive habits into your life. Try one new habit each week, or if that's too difficult, one new habit each month. The harder you work at this, the better the outcome. All we are trying to do here is retrain your thinking patterns to work in a proactive, positive way for you, enabling you to move more freely in your life.

KICKING BAD THINKING HABITS

Creating freeways out of dirt roads! The biggest challenge that we face in trying to change our negative, destructive dialogue into positive optimistic, encouraging dialogue

"In order to move forward, we have to create new thought patterns."

is that it can take time to kick the old habit and create the new one.

We may have inherited our thoughts and beliefs from all sorts of people at different points in our lives . . . some of them as far back as early childhood, so we're not even aware of them. We've formed bad habits that self-activate, creating feelings and responses within us as we go about our everyday lives. In order to move forward, we have to create new thought patterns.

I often use the analogy of the pathways in the brain being like the highway systems on our roads. Freeways are the speediest ways to travel. Our habitual thoughts fly down the freeways of our minds. Traveling on minor roads and paths with their potholes and blind curves is a slower, more difficult way to get from A to B, and the new thought patterns that we need to create may have to take a slower route at first. When we change our thought patterns, it can be just like beginning to create a new road; in fact, it's like going back to horseback travel over fields and hills. When we create a new habitual thought pattern, we often have to really concentrate in the first instance, and there are always times when we will fall down or forget where we are going. As we continue to practice running the thought through our minds repeatedly, however, it eventually becomes ingrained. I'm fortunate to be surrounded by people who teach affirmations, but I am human just like you, and I'll admit that at first I found it tough. The bottom line is that if you really want to make changes, especially if they are fundamental ones, you are going to have to work hard at it. This is what really makes the difference. You can attend the best goal-setting seminars in the world, and have the most fantastic dreams and aspirations, however if you don't have the right beliefs and mind-set, you can forget the goal. It won't happen unless the beliefs you have about yourself are in alignment with the goal.

In this part of the book, I'm going to spend a good chunk of time explaining the art of doing affirmation statements. This is the one thing that will make the biggest difference. These tiny little statements are what fundamentally change lives. I have changed my thoughts from believing:

• *I am a bad mom because I work.*
• *I am ugly and I hate my face.*
• *I am out of control with my life.*
• *I am useless.*
• *I am depressed.*

to

• *I am a great mom—I am creative, loving, and gentle with Liberty.*
• *I like my face—I am attractive, and people remind me of this each day.*
• *I am totally in control with my life—I know exactly where I am going.*
• *I do so much good in the world—my purpose helps many people find hope.*
• *I feel fantastic, and I live life to the fullest. I am very lucky.*

My life is not a random event that is determined by chance. It's something that I can take control of . . . if I want to. When I am in a one-on-one situation with people, I can clearly and quickly detect what they are experiencing in their lives by gently questioning them and listening to what they are saying. Their words are an outward expression of their thoughts.

For example, here are some beliefs or affirmation statements that will keep someone's chances of finding a new relationship pretty low.

- *I'm never approached by men/women.*
- *I am never lucky in relationships.*
- *People always walk all over me.*
- *I never meet anyone when I go out.*
- *I don't deserve someone anyway.*
- *I'm uninteresting or dull.*
- *I'm too shy to speak to anyone.*
- *I've been hurt, and it's not going to happen to me again.*
- *I can't stand men/women; they're all the same.*

In contrast, the following are positive beliefs and affirmation statements that will attract new partners into someone's life:

- *People talk to me when I go out. I look sexy, keep my head up and eyes open, and smile.*
- *People are interested in my life. I have so much to offer.*
- *I am really attractive. People notice me.*
- *I chat easily with people I haven't met before.*
- *Someone will be so lucky to meet me. I'm a great catch.*
- *I'm moving into my new glorious future. I can't wait to experience joy.*
- *I am lucky in relationships. People treat me with respect.*

Can you see how these words, which don't even need to be said, give out a signal about what someone is thinking or feeling? People can sense what we are thinking or feeling. Self-confidence is an internal dialogue that oozes from our pores. It's vibrant, it's sexy, and it's attractive, and everyone wants a bit of it. It attracts opportunities, and it shouts when you don't even open your mouth. . . .

What's your internal dialogue like?

AFFIRMATIONS ARE JUST LIKE DIETS

I often describe the practice of affirmations as a bit like going on a diet. When we follow the eating plan and change our eating habits, then we lose weight. If we revert to our old eating habits, the weight piles back on.

Equally, if we read our new positive affirmation statements each day, we will begin to feel the positive changes in our emotions and see the positive impact in our lives. If we stop reading the new positive affirmations before the habit has kicked in, nothing will ever change. Our old, limiting, and negative thought patterns will dominate, and our feelings and habits will revert to the old ways.

There's no doubt that this takes commitment and discipline, and I'm going to try my best to help you build some techniques into your daily life to ensure that you have the discipline you need. I wish I could make it happen for you, but I can't, so you're going to have to give it your best shot.

WHY DIETS DON'T WORK!

I remember going along to a dieting class after I gave birth to Liberty. In the first week, I crept into the back row of the dingy, packed hall. I got in just in time, and as I sat down, the doors were locked. The sinners who thought they could take this form of discipline lightly by being late were firmly locked out! I realized that this was a strict regime, and if you wanted to lose the weight, you had to stick to the rules.

I anxiously anticipated what they were going to tell me to do. The lady who took the stage looked like a pretty normal kind of woman; however, her manner was very firm and a bit godlike. She could be funny, too, which reassured me that she actually was human! She offered an unforgiving talk about how the latest breakfast bar may say less than 5 percent fat; however, the truth was something quite different. Marketers were out to trick us. We, the dieting population, were their biggest prey. Her role was to protect us, to educate us in the unmistakable pitfalls of dieting. She was there to remind us that if we listened to her, if we obeyed the rules and stuck to the *plan,* just like she had done, we too could lose weight.

As I looked around the room, I saw thin women in pencil skirts in the front rows: the trophy girls who had done it and were now beaming with confidence. They had achieved their target weight and were using this weekly ritualistic program as a crutch to ensure that they didn't fall back onto the slippery slope of excess baggage. In the back rows there were the diehards, the bigger ladies still carrying a few pounds too many. Week after week they were coming in to be weighed, in the hopes of losing at least one or two pounds.

I left after the first session feeling excited; my hunger pangs had been annihilated by the lecture about good and bad food. I held my little manual—my diet plan that reminded me of what I was to eat, how much I was to eat, and when I was to eat—tightly in my hand and headed back home.

In the manual, I was offered little treats to reward myself every day, and if I followed the *plan,* She Who Was Godlike and Had to Be Obeyed said that I would reach my target weight in about eight weeks. I went back to the group for another five weeks, excited about the prospect of standing on the little set of scales that had the loudest voice in the world! These scales screamed to everyone in the room whether they'd succeeded or failed that week. If we succeeded, a bell would ring, people would smile and often clap, we'd feel proud and be motivated to stick to the *plan,* and we'd come back next week for more of the same!

I would often stand in the line to be weighed and listen to the women chatting. Some were nervous and just stood in silent anticipation, some talked of their Saturday nights out when they had fallen off the path—they'd had an Indian korma and six glasses of wine, and starved themselves on Sunday. Here they were on Monday evening, hoping that they would scrape by on the scales. Even if they hadn't lost the two pounds they wanted to, they prayed that they hadn't put on any weight.

When we stuck to the *plan,* we'd have improved confidence and self-esteem, great gaps in the waistbands of our jeans, and in extreme cases, the absolute need to buy a whole new wardrobe of smaller, sexier, trendier clothes that would make us feel absolutely amazing. My downfall began one Friday. It had been a tough day at work; there were emotional tensions in the office, and the team decided that to feel better we should head over to the bar for a little drink after work. The voice of She Who Was Godlike and Had to Be Obeyed ran through my mind. For the first time in six weeks, I wanted a big glass of Australian Ruby Shiraz. The *plan* said that I had to have a white wine and soda to ensure keeping my wits about me. Three glasses and lots of giggling later, I was standing at the bar ordering four bags of chips and two packets of nuts and another round of red wine. The *plan* had gone out of my mind. The hunger gremlins were in again, and I was falling off the path fast!

On the way home from the wine bar, I passed the chip shop. I love fish and chips and hadn't eaten any for what felt like an eternity. I was so hungry that I thought on this one occasion that I'd break the rules a bit. I'd make up for it the next day, so She Who Had to Be Obeyed would not need to yell at me!

The next day I woke up hungover and hungry. My partner was having a couple of sweet rolls. I thought maybe I'd have one, then on reflection I thought I'd have a couple! By lunchtime, I was so far off the *plan* that I thought I may as well have an Indian korma that night and some lovely red wine. My old habits were kicking in fast, and my palate was readjusting to my old ways. By Monday, I was too frightened to go to the class. I missed it once and thought that I would catch up with my points and go back the following week. That never happened . . . I never became a trophy girl. I never lost the 30 pounds that I wanted to. I never bought the whole new wardrobe of smaller, sexier clothes. The reality was that I stopped following the *plan,* and the weight went back on. Six months later, I was at the bar with one of my friends and they asked me if I'd ever gone to a dieting organization. I said yes, I had . . . but it didn't work!

The bottom line is that they *do* work, if we follow the *plan.* If we don't follow the *plan* and go back to our old habits, we will never lose weight!

CHAPTER EIGHT

The Five Magical Ingredients

How to ensure that positive affirmations really work:

If we really understand positive affirmations and practice them religiously, they absolutely do work— but many people don't manage to do them successfully. They try them and find that it's hard work to keep doing them . . . and soon they find themselves giving up. I do affirmations all the time, but sometimes I revert to old thought patterns and behaviors . . . that's because I'm human, and from time to time it's okay.

My classic downfall is that I often find myself hating my face, which is bizarre because people compliment me all the time, and when they do, I commit the deadly sin of bouncing the compliment back to them, telling them not to be silly. I do this because I have a deep-seated belief that my face is really unattractive. If I'm struggling with something in my life, it will have an immediate impact on my confidence and I have to start all over again.

So every six months or so I write up lots of little Post-it notes and stick them on my mirrors at home with reminders—accelerators, as I call them—of who calls me attractive and why they say what they say. Within a few days, I begin to be gentle with myself again.

I have little sticky notes that say:

Today I release the need to judge my face and my body.
You have beautiful eyes, you have a pretty face, and you are complimented every day.
You are unique and everything about you is unique.
I release the need to compare myself to anyone else.
I am perfect exactly as I am.

Eventually I begin to believe that I am perfect exactly as I am, and it makes me feel much better. The trouble is that if I clean my mirror and take down the sticky notes, then the beliefs begin to go back to the old ones!

To ensure that positive affirmation statements work effectively, we have to make sure that we follow five magical rules: Affirmations need to be written as the opposite of your current belief, they have to be written in the present tense, they must only contain positive language, they must be written in a powerful tone for you, and they must only be personal and about you. You must practice them every day to reprogram your brain.

Rule Number One

Think the opposite of what you actually believe.

When we write positive affirmation statements, we are trying to reprogram our brain into a new way of thinking. To do this, we need to delete or override the old thought pattern with the opposite of the current belief. Remember the lemon exercise! Our brains will believe and react to whatever we feed them.

Let me show you some examples:

1. Someone believes that they are fat and thinks that diets don't work for them, but they really want to lose weight. They could use the following affirmations: *I love the feeling of being slim and attractive; I eat only fresh fruit and vegetables each day; I go to the gym three times a week; each day my body looks better and better.*

2. Someone has been hurt by an ex-partner in what was a difficult relationship, and may be frightened of going into future relationships. They could use these affirmations: *I move into my new glorious future; I am open to new possibilities; I have loved and learned; I'm excited by the prospect of a full, warm, loving relationship.*

3. Someone who feels they are being walked all over by their boss, and who creates tension in the office. They could use the affirmations: *I go to the office each day feeling relaxed, and as I interact with others, I am always neutral; I have harmonious relationships at work.*

Rule Number Two

Think in the present tense.

Talking in the present tense when we haven't actually achieved the outcome is one of the most difficult parts of practicing affirmation statements. If we say we are going to do something in the future, then all of our responses will be geared up to respond at a later date. Let me give you an example:

In about a year's time, I will definitely move to a new house.

When you think this thought, it gives your subconscious responses a get-out clause to ensure that:

- you don't have to look for a new house just yet;
- you don't have to worry about finding out about the mortgage arrangements now; and
- you don't have to worry about packing up and arranging a move.

It is highly probable that when you keep the option in the future, you might just keep pushing this goal farther and farther away, and maybe you will never, ever make the move.

When we change the tense of an affirmation statement to the present tense, our subconscious mind begins to go to work and we might just find that the outcome happens more quickly than we expect. For example: "I am now in the process of moving to my new house in the country." This new thought in the present tense drives our actions. Now:

• your mind is always looking for options, scanning the newspapers and watching out for new houses in the country;
• just in case the right place comes up you might check out the mortgage situation; and
• you may begin to do some clearing out and mentally start packing.

Here are some examples of statements written in the future tense and some options on how to change them.

In a few years I am going to set up my own exciting new business in ceramics.
When will you really get around to this?

I am going to begin to eat fresh nutritious healthy food.
When will you do this—next week?

I will make quality time just for me.
When will you actually do it?

In the present tense, we can change these to read:

I am now in the process of setting up my exciting new ceramics business.

I now only eat fresh, nutritious, healthy food each day.

I now make quality time for me—it's essential and feels great.

Case Study

In one of my workshops, a lady challenged me about the concept of using the present tense when she wanted to move to a new house in the future. She had lived in the same house for 25 years, and had always dreamed that she might move to a little house in the country one day. When we explored why she hadn't done it so far, she had no real reasons.

She didn't want to write her statement down in the present tense. She realized that if she wrote the statement in the now, a beautiful home might come up, and she might find herself in a position where she would have to move faster than she thought.

This was a real problem, as she had a house full of clutter that would take weeks if not months to pack up! I asked her, "What if you found the house of your dreams next week?

Could you find a way to get packed up and move?" Of course she could, but the belief that she couldn't get packed up in time was blocking her dream.

If she hadn't changed the tense of her affirmation, she might have stayed in that cluttered house for the rest of her life—but she moved to the most beautiful house in the country five months later!

Rule Number Three

Feed your brain positive language.

When we make up positive affirmation statements, we must ensure that the language is absolutely right. Remember the lemon exercise: Whatever we tell our brain, whether it's true or false, our brain will automatically send a response. Let's take someone who really wants to lose weight. Their affirmation might be the following:

I am now on a diet and I'm going to lose so much weight.

In this statement, the brain hears the word *diet*, which for most people triggers thoughts like *I want chocolate, this is hard work, I might fail . . .* or *Get me food now!* The word *diet* makes us feel under pressure.

When we are constructing positive affirmations, we need to be very careful that the words and language actually send a feel-good sensation to our brain! For example:

I now eat lots of fresh, healthy fruit and nuts, and this makes me feel great!
I now eat low-fat healthy food, lots of big salads, and interesting fruits.
I always take the healthy option, and this makes me feel energized and in control.

With each of these statements, the brain focuses on something that excites it and makes it feel optimistic about the outcome.

Here are some examples of words that create a negative response in our body and need to be changed.

My life is no longer a nightmare—
I'm loving every day!
I am over my abusive relationship—
I'm ready to move on now!
I no longer have headaches—I feel great . . .

Options for changing these statements may be . . .

My life is great—as of today I am loving every moment.
I am moving into my new glorious future—I feel good.
I am healthy and feel well every day!

PINK, SPOTTY KANGAROOS!
Try doing this.

I want you to think about anything except great big, pink, yellow-spotted kangaroos jumping up and down on huge trampolines. Think about anything except the big, pink kangaroos with yellow spots, jumping up and down. Try to focus your mind, and think about anything else.

What did you think about? Did you think about big, pink, spotty kangaroos on trampolines?

The purpose of this exercise is to show you that whatever you think about over and over will dominate your thoughts. For example, if you constantly think about weight and dieting, all you will think about is weight, dieting, chocolate, and food! If you think constantly about the fact that you should not feel guilty about visiting your parents only once a year, you will perpetuate the feelings of guilt.

Be very careful when you set up your affirmations to ensure that the language is not going to make you feel bad or perpetuate what you don't want. When

you write positive affirmations, *always* ensure that the language is focused on the positive stuff.

Rule Number Four

You can only influence your life.

So often we want other people to change. We focus all our energy and attention on how we can get them to change. The only person that you can change is you. We cannot change other people—they will change only if they actually want to change!

If we can change our own responses, this will make life feel a little easier. We humans are equipped with many emotions, and we naturally react emotionally to the behavior of others. We get wound up, frustrated, angry, hurt, and upset when people treat us a particular way.

Here's an example of an affirmation that wouldn't work:

From today on, my boss will treat me with respect.

"Whatever you think about over and over will dominate your thoughts."

The bottom line here is that you cannot change your boss's responses; however, you can actually change your own. You can make a decision in a second that your boss's responses are no longer going to affect you in the same way; you may decide to always remain in a neutral mode when your boss looks for a reaction.

Case Study

Alison used to work in a large insurance company. Each day the boss would practice his bully-boy tactics on everyone in the office. Alison used to leave work each day emotionally drained after being put through the mill.

Once Alison practiced the art of affirmation, she realized that she could flick the switch and turn off her emotional responses in this hurtful situation.

Her affirmation was:

All of my relationships are harmonious. I always behave in a neutral fashion with each individual I interact with.

Alison read this affirmation every day for weeks and repeated it over and over in her mind. The situation stopped affecting her, and eventually the boss's response began to change. After some time, he didn't bother with Alison because she wasn't giving him any response.

You have the power to flick that switch!

Here are some other examples of affirmations that wouldn't be particularly effective:

- *My partner buys me flowers once a week to show me how much he loves me.*
- *My daughter now expresses her feelings to me.*
- *My mother is making a full recovery.*

To turn these around into positive, optimistic affirmations for you that will take away the pressure and make life a bit easier, you could change them to:

• *I accept my partner exactly as he is.*
• *I am the best mom I can be. I listen to and talk with my daughter. I release the need for her to conform to my expectations. I accept her exactly as she is.*
• *I accept that Mom is 85, and she will fight for her life if she wants to. I accept her decisions. This is her life and she knows her own limitations.*

When we turn these statements around, we often let go of huge inner struggles. It can be such a liberating feeling.

Don't let anyone get to you.

From now on, I take nothing personally.

This is such a powerful affirmation. So often the way people treat us says much more about them than it does about us. Sometimes people treat us disrespectfully, they try to walk over us, and they are dominating and aggressive. It's very difficult not to be affected or to take this kind of behavior personally.

A dear friend of mine was married to an angry and aggressive man. They are separated now; however, he regularly calls her and reminds her that she is a useless mother, that she is unclean, and that she is irresponsible. I know this woman well, and she is gentle, kind, bright, and incredibly responsible. She has a wonderful home and a beautiful son. She says that each time her ex is rude and yells at her, she just ignores what he says . . . however, a few days later the words begin to ring in her head again. She begins to doubt herself and then she gives herself a good talking to as she reminds herself that her ex is the voice reinforcing what her gremlins are shouting!

"Some people are insecure on the inside, and their only way of assuming more control of their lives is to bully or harass others."

Some people are insecure on the inside, and their only way of assuming some control in their lives is to bully or harass others. Often the only way to stop feeling frightened is to imagine that they have no control over you. In your mind, tell yourself every day . . . *I can deal with you. You have a real problem. Poor you!*

You might want to imagine that when they speak, they have a squeaky voice or imagine them naked or standing in a tutu. We really do have an inner ability to disable their impact on our emotions.

Rule Number Five

Have a strong, powerful dialogue.

Like everything in life, different styles of affirmations work for different people. Some people like them to be short and snappy—they find that the shorter the affirmation, the easier they remember it, and that works for them. Others find that descriptive, goal-focused affirmations work best.

As we work through this section on affirmations, please become aware of what works best for you.

Here are some examples of powerful, short, and snappy affirmations:

- *I am slim, and fit, and I love my body.*
- *I am a positive and optimistic person.*
  - *I move into my glorious new future with ease.*
    - *I feel great and am in perfect health.*
    - *I am gorgeous and loved.*
    - *I accept myself exactly as I am, and from now on I am gentle with myself.*

Here are some variations in a more descriptive style:

- *I eat healthy, nutritious food each day; this has a powerful impact on my body. I love the way that I feel, and I love the new me in the mirror.*
- *I have a positive, optimistic outlook. I spend time with lots of positive people, and I read and listen to uplifting books and tapes every day. The impact upon my life is fantastic; I feel great.*
- *I am excited about today, I move into this new chapter of my life with ease. I have loved and learned, and I am excited about loving again.*
- *I am a fit and energetic person, and I go to the gym each day; this makes me feel amazing. The endorphins flush through my body, healing and repairing it. I feel tremendous and am in perfect health.*
- *I am attractive. I love the responses that I feel from everyone around me. When I go out, I lift my head high, smile, and I'm noticed by lots of attractive men and/or women.*

ACCELERATE YOUR PROGRESS

Now that you know the rules for constructing affirmations, I'd like to introduce a little technique that enables you to reinforce your new belief, making it more powerful and more believable. I remember finding it a little difficult to believe that by changing my thoughts around, writing them in the present tense, and repeating them as often as I possibly could, I could actually begin to change how I felt and shape my destiny.

My biggest challenge was that I didn't actually believe some of my affirmations. While it's true that our brain will respond to whatever we tell it, habitual thought patterns can be hard to shift. When I began to teach, I watched people struggle with affirmations, so I invented a little technique that made them much more believable and effective.

The technique is to back up every affirmation statement with a set of support statements, or accelerators. For example:

• Compliments that you have received in the past
• Memories to support the affirmation
  • Experiences from your past that support this affirmation
    • The fine details that will excite you about the affirmation
• The benefits of the outcome of the affirmation
  • The actions that you will take to support this affirmation

I remember being asked to look into a mirror every day and say, "I love you, Dawn." I found this so difficult. I hated my face at the time, and I also hated me because I was unhappy and living out of alignment with the desires of my heart and soul. If I had used accelerators with this statement, I feel it would have been more powerful. Let me show you exactly how they work.

"I love you . . ."
  • *You deserve to live life to the fullest.*
  • *Remember when you were so happy— you deserve that time again.*
  • *You are beautiful—people tell you how pretty you are every day.*
    • *You are spirited and funny and deserve to let that energy flow.*
  • *If you love and respect yourself, you will be happy again.*

If you do a similar affirmation each day in the mirror, your feelings of self-loathing will begin to dissolve. Different accelerators will have a different impact for each of us:

• *I now attend salsa classes on Tuesdays and Fridays.*

• *I now attend yoga classes on Sundays and Wednesdays.*
• *I feel calm and peaceful.*
• *I feel slim, fit, and healthy.*
• *I eat nutritious, creative salads.*
• *My fruit bowl is full of fresh, delicious fruit.*
• *I feel energized and less stressed.*
• *I feel sexy and sensual.*
• *I love myself and respect my body.*

I advise you to support your affirmation with at least five or six of these statements. Can you see how by forming the accelerators, the desire to believe and stick to the affirmation increases?

PRACTICE MAKES PERFECT

As I mentioned at the beginning of this chapter, these affirmations *will not work* unless we practice retraining the brain to think in a new way. To help you do this, here are some creative and fun ways to do positive affirmations.

Have you ever recorded something on tape and heard the *old* music play through the *new* recording? You have to tape it again and again until the old recording has faded away. That's what we have to do here. Every day we need to rerecord over the old, limiting, and restrictive dialogue in our brain until we can't hear the words anymore.

We need to make the new positive, encouraging, and optimistic dialogue a very clear recording!

The more ingrained the old messages are, the harder we need to work at the rerecording stage. You judge how hard you need to work at this—if your gremlins scream so loudly that they stop you from doing what you want to do in your life, then you need to practice at least four times a day.

GET CREATIVE

We each have different ways of absorbing information. Here are some ideas for you to create fun ways to practice your affirmations.

Tip: Our brains love color, and when we do our affirmations in bright colors, maybe using illustrations or patterns, we stimulate the brain more than by simply reading a list. If we put some real effort into creating our affirmations, the impact will be greater. Make some time to create one of the following options to do your affirmations, and don't start until you have invested in a pack of brightly colored felt-tip pens (or borrowed your kids'!).

"... practice
retraining the brain
to think in a new way."

THE POWER BOOK

Buy a little book that will fit into your hand-bag, jacket pocket, or briefcase, and fill the pages with affirmations in bright colors. At every opportunity, take the little book out and read it. Put other things in this little book, like compliments people have given you, and photos of friends or family. Make this your little feel-good book that you carry around. Update it with feelings of achievement as your affirmations begin to work for you.

CREATE AN AFFIRMATIONS SHEET

The brain loves color. Write some affirmations in different colors on a piece of paper. Have the paper color copied, stick it everywhere you can think of, and read it each day. Once a month, review and update your affirmations. Put a reminder in colored ink in your calendar!

RECORD YOURSELF

Record your affirmations onto tape and listen to them each day as you drive to work, or play them as you do housework. As you listen to them, make an effort to absorb them with passion. Maybe you could say "YES!" every time you hear a new affirmation. This will keep your attention on the affirmation and stop it from becoming too familiar. Rerecord some new ones every two to three weeks to keep your mind interested and stimulated.

SING YOUR AFFIRMATIONS

Make your affirmations into rhymes, and sing them over and over out loud. (This probably works best alone!) This is a great way to re-program the subconscious. Again, to keep your interest alive, make up some new ones about once a month. Write yourself reminders in your diary!

PAINT YOUR WALLS

If you really want to be wacky, paint some of your affirmations about your new perception of life onto your bathroom walls in gold paint. You can do this really tastefully . . . especially if you live alone! Why not paint some encouraging ones on your kids' walls, too?

MORNING RITUAL

Each day, get up 15 minutes before everyone else. Light a candle, sit down, relax, and read your affirmations. Set your mind into a positive frame for the whole day. You might want to repeat this around bedtime, too.

Tip: Make your first affirmation this one:
I love doing these affirmations that make me feel excited about my future. Today I am open to all the new, wonderful experiences that life has to offer me.

LET'S GET YOU INTO TRAINING!

How could you build this daily ritual of retraining your thinking patterns into your life? At what points in the day could you build the habit in? Here are some examples of ideas that have worked for other people.

Mirror Affirmations

Write up some really colorful Post-it notes and stick them all over the mirrors in the house. Every time you look in the mirror, read the affirmations.

Calendar Affirmations

Make a list at the front of your calendar. Each morning before you begin your daily work, read the list. Make this your habit, every day.

Restroom Affirmations

Make a colorful list of affirmations that you take with you every time you take a bathroom break. This will ensure that you are training five or six times a day! Alternately, if you are at home, stick your lists on the bathroom walls and read them there if you can!

Toothbrush Affirmations

Pop a list of colorful affirmations next to your toothbrush or on the bathroom mirror, and every time you brush your teeth, read your affirmations.

Teatime Affirmations

Keep a list of your affirmations beside the kettle, and as it boils, read bright, colorful affirmations over and over.

Driving Affirmations

In the car, keep a list on your dashboard. When you get into the car in the morning, read the list, and then read it again as you are about to get out at the end of the day.

Bedtime Affirmations

Read your affirmations before you go to sleep every night.

Ready-Made Affirmations

Take your pick to design your life.

Here is a selection of ready-made affirmations. Read them slowly and feel the impact on your mind, body, and spirit as you allow these new thoughts to enter your mind. Choose selections that really fit with the way you would love to be living your life, and repeat them as often as you can in whatever way works best for you. I suggest that you write at least four actions or accelerators for each affirmation to bring it to life, and in turn into your reality. Good luck! Practice and feel the fantastic effects of these affirmations.

If it takes a little time for these affirmations to penetrate, that's okay, You have developed your thought patterns over a number of years. If it doesn't fit right now, come back when it's right for you. You are a precious human being, and I really want you to begin loving yourself—and that means being patient and gentle with yourself. . . .

From this moment on, I say yes to life.
When I say yes to life,
LIFE SAYS YES TO ME.

＊

I am FOCUSED on breathing new
energy and enthusiasm into my
life to make every day special!

＊

From now on, I make
a real effort to love life even
more than I did yesterday.

＊

I have the POWER IN THIS MOMENT
to make some POSITIVE CHANGES
in my life.

＊

I have the power within me
to HEAL MY BODY. From today on,
I do what I love.

＊

Today I decide TO BE GENTLE with myself.
Being GENTLE HELPS ME HEAL.

Life feels fantastic
when I make an effort to live it!

＊

I have the POWER today to change
my life for the better forever.

＊

TODAY I GRASP my dream.
It's only a matter of making the choice.

＊

I HAVE THE POWER TODAY
to let go the baggage and the pain
of my past experiences.

＊

I say yes to LIFE TODAY.
This feels fantastic.

＊

From NOW ON, I choose to FALL IN LOVE
with my partner all over again.
I make the effort to recreate the SPARKLE.

＊

MY partner and I NOW create
a magical life together.

Our FUTURE IS WHAT WE
CHOOSE IT TO BE.

*

My inner child is desperate to be set free.
I hold the key to playing with life again.
I begin TODAY.

*

I am a unique and wonderful human being.
I rejoice in my uniqueness and
accept myself exactly as I am.

*

I love and respect my body.
I am healthy and filled with energy.
I feel amazing as I feed my body
healthy, nutritious food.

*

It is my divine right to be happy in this life.
I respect the voice of my inner child.
I TAKE CONTROL TODAY, and
I deserve this.

*

I release the past, and from this moment on I
move into my new future. This feels fantastic.
I deserve this.

*

I love and nurture my
inner child and feed her/him
with lots of fun, creativity, and love.
This will ensure that I feel happy.

I FORGIVE MYSELF. It's all I can do;
I can't change the past.

*

My mind is open to the future.
I WELCOME CHANGE, and as I do,
I grow and feel free.

*

From this moment on, I release the need to criticize
myself and others. I now focus on the positive in myself
and others. This feels great!

*

From now on, I have the courage to speak up for
myself, as I deserve to be heard. I am as valuable as the
next human being. This sets me free.

*

I release the need to control others and accept that I
can only do my best, and that's okay.

*

Today I CHOOSE ONLY to feed my brain
positive food!

*

I now only speak positively about people.
I'm breaking old habits.

I spend time with my positive, optimistic friends and family. Friends are like the best vitamins—they make me feel great!

*

I nurture my creative spirit by sharing my ideas only with people who will encourage and support me.

*

The pain of the past was an old friend.
Today I choose to let this go.
I have this POWER within me NOW.

*

TODAY I set myself free as I
TAKE CONTROL and
deal with what I need to in life.

*

My lungs are clean and healthy.
My breath smells fresh, and my clothes smell clean. I feel so much healthier!

*

I commit to recharging my batteries,
to ENERGIZE MY LIFE.

AFFIRMATIONS FOR KIDS

I wrote this section to help you begin to work on affirmations with your children. I have a list of affirmations on my fridge, and at breakfast time, Liberty and I read through them. It's a great way to teach your children to understand themselves, and it really helps them manage their emotions. These affirmations can be adapted and changed, depending on what's going on in your kids' lives.

Remember to be gentle with yourself and your child; you won't be able to change everything about your child's perceptions and reactions with affirmations. Genetics play a big part in your kid's behavior, but by using affirmations you can really begin to help your child understand the impact of their thoughts on their lives.

This exercise cost me a tuna panini, a raspberry Frappucino®, and some bracelets from Claire's Accessories.

Thanks to Liberty (age 8) for putting these together for me . . .

Love, Mom xxx

I love myself, and
I am always honest about how I feel.
This makes me feel happy inside.
This makes my parent(s) happy, too!

I respect others.
This means people will be nice to me.
I will be happy because I have friends,
    and I will feel good inside.

I am important.
Even though I am a child, I deserve to be heard.
It's always important that people know the truth.
I grow up to be happy.

I am a unique and special human being.
Everyone is different; no one is the same.
I feel happy being different, because
    different people make the world an interesting place.

I easily tell people how I feel.
It means I won't worry anymore.
I feel good inside my heart.
I now make friends with everyone again.

I always think of other people's feelings
    when I say things.
It makes me feel good inside my body.
It's nice to respect people in a good way,
    and people won't hurt inside anymore.

I do my homework as soon as I come home
from school. This means I can play when it's done.
I don't worry about it all night,
    and my parent(s) don't nag me!

I enjoy trying new things, and
    this means I won't miss out on good things.
This stops me from being bored.
Always after I try, I make new friends and
    I am not frightened anymore.

I enjoy school.
I always do my best, that's what's important.
I am good at different things and that's okay, because
    different people are good at different things.

TRIED-AND-TESTED AFFIRMATIONS! THE CASE STUDIES

I know lots of single men and women who would like to find a new partner, yet when it comes to going out to a place where they might meet someone, they return home not having spoken to even one new person! They go out with the intention of getting acquainted with someone new, but are thinking all the wrong thoughts, which in turn affects how they appear to others when they actually meet new people.

You need to become aware of the way you are thinking and behaving when you go to dinner parties, bars, or clubs. You might be expecting some kind of outcome, but the way you look and behave toward others doesn't suggest that this is what you want, and nobody even notices that you are there. You might believe that there is never anyone interesting around, or if there is, they don't talk to you . . . and if you stare into your drink, keep your head down, and never smile, is it any wonder that you never meet anyone new?!

Case Study: Shirley the Pussycat

After a workshop in which almost 70 percent of the people attending were single, I suggested we go out to a bar en masse. The challenge was to master everyone's internal dialogue to ensure that it was positive and upbeat. Upon entering the bar, we would create such a stir that everyone would be speaking to someone new before the end of the evening. We were definitely going to get a response! Everyone had to think of an animal that they thought was really sexy, and in their minds, they had to become this animal and act out some of its characteristics. Sounds crazy, but it works!

Shirley, who had been single for about ten years, chose *I am a pussycat.*

• *When I'm out, I smile at everyone who looks at me.*
• *I stand tall and I am sexy.*
• *I move gracefully.*
• *I look around everywhere I go.*

Thank God she didn't say it all out loud! That night as she began to repeat it in her mind, she oozed confidence, and on the train home she ended up talking to a man five years her junior. She felt that she had found a magic potion!

Case Study:

Jon's Sexy Bum

My friend Jonny came along to one of my workshops. At the workshop he realized that the only area in his life where goal-setting wasn't working was in relationships, and when we inspected his internal dialogue, I understood why. Jonny believed that he was unattractive and fat. I couldn't believe that this was what he thought of himself. He is so immaculate, handsome, and strong . . . I'd never thought of him as fat! We worked on some new affirmations, and by the end of the workshop, he was excited about the prospect of giving his new affirmations a try!

On Saturday night he went to a club. As he walked up to the bar, he repeated in his mind, *I am absolutely gorgeous, I have a sexy bum, and I'm oozing attractiveness.* He was astounded when someone came up to him and said, "You are absolutely gorgeous, and you have the most sexy bum!" Jonny phoned me the next day. He said that he couldn't believe what had happened. He was absolutely amazed and had found a new way to get what he wanted in life!

It makes sense that if you are thinking negative and destructive thoughts about yourself, people will pick up on what you are thinking. Thoughts carry energy like electricity, and when they are positively charged, people will respond accordingly. Your body language and posture give you away.

"Your body langauge and posture give you away."

CHAPTER NINE

The Mind-Body Connection

Seven years ago, it was a real eye-opener to me to find out that how I was feeling mentally and emotionally was having a profound effect on my state of health. I can remember reading for the first time that all sorts of illnesses and ailments are often connected to our state of mind. For you, too, this may be a revelation. The case studies in this chapter show that what is going on in your life and how you are handling things is undoubtedly having an impact on your mental and physical health.

MIND YOUR LANGUAGE

When we think back to the lemon exercise (page 64), we realize that by just imagining a lemon in our mouth, we can activate our internal pharmacy. That simple exercise speaks volumes to me. It tells me that whatever I am thinking is having a biochemical effect on my body. If the thoughts are positive and constructive, then the impact will be healthy; however, if they are negative, then the response may be the same. When we do the head-turning exercise (page 65) and imagine and visualize that we can turn our heads farther and we do, again this shows me that the thoughts we are sending to our brain are having an impact on our body. In this instance, the chemical reaction that is happening in our body is relaxing the muscle to increase our range of vision.

As we begin to accept the impact our mind is having on our body, we must start to consider exactly what thoughts and language are in our heads every day. In the section on affir-mations, hopefully you began to recognize the real importance of thinking and speaking with the right language. Awareness of this fact can have a really profound effect on the way you feel every day.

Do you ever find yourself saying any of the following?

- I'm always unwell.
- I always get headaches.
- I feel exhausted all the time.
- My life is a nightmare.
- I hate my life.
- I feel depressed.
- I always get colds in the winter.
- I'm a worrier.
- I'm miserable.
- This will never change.

These statements are all sending messages to your brain, which responds to whatever you feed it, and, in turn, this is affecting your body. So be aware of *your* language, and listen to other people's language.

EXERCISE
Just for this week, pay attention to the people around you as they talk about their health. Listen to their language, and see for yourself if you can detect a connection.

WARNING
Although you may want to reeducate people about their thoughts and language as soon as you hear how they are thinking, hold back if you can—either show them this section in the book or lend the book to them when you're finished.

When I realized that my thoughts and beliefs were having a great impact on my health, my immediate reaction was to change the way I was thinking and speaking. I began to read as much as I could about the subject and was astounded by what I found out. Many doctors still do not believe in or take account of this mind-body connection, although there is increased awareness of the power and effectiveness of alternative and complementary therapies and remedies. The challenge in the field of science is that to have anything accepted or recognized, it must be proven scientifically by clearly showing the facts.

We still know so little about human beings and the world we live in. I was amazed to read that in 1961, a Nobel Prize was won for working out just exactly how we hear; in 1967, the prize was won for working out how we see; and in the year 2003, scientists are still battling in labs all over the world to try to work out how we smell. In our lives, we make lots of assumptions about how we do things, when in fact we actually know so little. Scientists are still mystified by how the body works, and doctors learn about facts that have been scientifically tried, tested, and proven in the history of science. Experienced doctors and family doctors in small communities can often make a diagnosis based on historical information, trends, and knowledge that they have personally accumulated over the years. Most of the time they know only what they have learned and often they have to play a guessing game by associating symptoms with the nearest possible disease or disorder.

IRRITABLE BOWEL SYNDROME … OR IS IT?

My friend John was feeling very depressed—he'd had a stomach complaint for three years and spent a lot of time going to see doctors and consultants at the hospital. He was tired of the continuing feelings of depression, and the hospitals could not diagnose his condition. Eventually it was diagnosed as irritable bowel syndrome. This was the closest the medical profession could come up with based on the symptoms that John was experiencing. Alison, another friend of ours, introduced him to a lovely lady called Cherry from Perthshire in Scotland. Cherry was an alternative therapist and did a number of tests with John. Within three days, his stomach complaint disappeared. Cherry diagnosed his complaint as a strain of wheat intolerance.

A PLANT THAT CURES

Dr. Joel L. Swerdlow went to Madagascar to write an article for *National Geographic* magazine, the result of which is a wonderful book called *Nature's Medicine: Plants that Heal*. In the introduction, Joel talks about his brother, Paul, a doctor who was diagnosed with myelogeneous leukemia. As he spent time with him in the hospital, Joel witnessed Paul's treatment firsthand and knew that modern medicine didn't have a lot to offer him. In his research, Joel learned that the Madagascar Rosy Periwinkle yielded chemicals that were said to cure acute lymphocytic leukemia. While his brother was dying, Joel hoped that a plant somewhere would contain the cure for Paul's leukemia. Paul died.

When Joel traveled to Madagascar, he learned of a healer who, it was said, could work miracles with cancer, using leaves that he called "killing little by little cancer." Philip, a fellow researcher, obtained some of these leaves from the healer, and they were sent off for tests to a pharmaceutical lab in Switzerland. The leaves were found to contain chemicals that were said to be effective in the treatment of the disease. The healer, fearful that his secrets might be stolen, would not give out any more leaves for further tests, but Philip was confident that he could go out with a botanist to pick some of his own. A second batch of leaves was sent to Switzerland and the results were negative! Was there some "magic ingredient" added by the healer himself? The question still remains a mystery.

This story is an example of what medical science doesn't know about disease and the possibility of healing. What worries me is that if a doctor says an illness is incurable or there is no hope, so many people take this information at face value and believe it, which has a negative impact on their health and leaves them feeling that they no longer have control in their lives.

Dr. Bernie Siegel, Louise L. Hay, Brandon Bays, and others in the field of mind-body healing, either personally or through their clients, have helped people reverse tumors and various forms of cancer. Science cannot explain why. I really do believe our minds have the potential to have a positive impact on our health.

UNCLE WILL

My friend Kirsty asked me if I could visit her uncle, who was 78 years old and had been diagnosed with leukemia. He had been told that if he didn't have treatment, he would have three months to live. He had to make a choice. I wasn't sure how I could help, but when I met Will, I knew within seconds that we would get on like a house on fire. He was a tall, slim man with a gentle nature. He had been a scientist, and his mind was still very active. I talked to him about the impact of mind over body, and he understood exactly where I was coming from. I asked Will to describe how he imagined the leukemia to be working inside his body. He described the white cells as little "Pac-Men" eating up the red cells and said that inside the marrow,

"Before long, Will became well again, and the doctors were baffled."

some of the cells were stuck. He said that some of the cells weren't growing the way they should have.

I asked him to create an imaginary scene in his mind and think about what he needed to do to ensure that the situation was reversed. He imagined that he needed to tend a garden and water the little cells to make them strong and healthy. I then wrote Will a visualization. I had never done this before, and both of us were experimenting, with no expectations on either side. Sometimes I think he just enjoyed doing the visualization, as if I were telling him a story ... he would always fall fast asleep and sometimes he'd snore! I'd watch over him and wish him all the healing in the world. When I wasn't there each day, he would lie down and listen to the visualization tape that I'd made him with some gentle music.

Before long, Will became well again, and the doctors were baffled. He passed away two years later.

The mind is a mysterious and powerful mechanism and science can only account for about 10 percent of its goings-on. When we believe in something strongly, we really can influence outcomes. We can make ourselves better, and we also have the ability to make ourselves worse.

THE QUEEN AND ST. COLUMBUS

I remember meeting a chief inspector of police on one of my programs in Edinburgh. The Chief Inspector told us about a time when she was working at St. Columbus Hospice, a cancer unit in London where on most days, a number of people passed away. The queen was visiting the hospice, and the chief inspector was there as part of the security team. On the week of the queen's visit, the mortality rates dropped to zero—everyone was waiting to see the queen; the week after her visit they went through the roof!

We all hear stories of people in the hospital who pass away in the night or when nobody is around. Does this mean that we can control when we die? I think that so often we put our lives into the hands of experts and expect them to have all the knowledge about how we can or can't get better. I'm not suggesting that doctors and professionals don't know what they are doing—in most cases they do a great job. Their work is based on knowledge and information that has been collected throughout the history of science and medicine. I believe that when we feel strongly about something, and when we listen to the body's intelligence, we can work out what we need to do to make changes to the way our bodies are reacting. Let's take a sore throat as a basic example. Our throats are our channel for communication, and sometimes when we find we have a sore throat, we might want to ask ourselves: *What am I holding back from saying to someone?* Try it, or the next time someone says that they have a sore throat, ask them if they aren't communicating what they really feel. I have been amazed at just how accurate this material is. Read the following list.

> "We might want to ask ourselves: *What am I holding back from saying to someone?*"

Here are some common ailments that may just get you thinking:

PROBLEM—Anxiety
PROBABLE CAUSE—Not trusting the flow and process of life
NEW THOUGHT—I love and approve of myself, and I trust the process of life. I am safe.

PROBLEM—Abnormal blood pressure
PROBABLE CAUSE—Long-standing emotional problems not solved; lack of love as a child
NEW THOUGHT—I jealously release the past. I am at peace. My life is a joy.

PROBLEM—Cystitis
PROBABLE CAUSE—Holding on to old ideas. Fear of letting go or being pissed off.
NEW THOUGHT—I comfortably and easily release the old and welcome the new in my life.

PROBLEM—Headaches
PROBABLE CAUSE—Invalidating the self; self-criticism or fear
NEW THOUGHT—I love and approve of myself. I see myself and what I do with eyes of love

(Excerpted from *You Can Heal Your Life,* with the kind permission of Louise L. Hay.)

I believe we must acknowledge our uniqueness and take responsibility for maintaining our own health and well-being. I believe passionately that when we assess how we are handling our everyday lives and begin to make some fundamental changes, there is a noticeable difference in the way we feel.

BERNIE SIEGEL ON CANCER

In *Love, Medicine & Miracles,* Dr. Bernie Siegel writes about his experience as a cancer surgeon. One day he became tired of cutting out cancer and decided to take on a consultant's job. He began to research the causes of cancer. He said that the people who visited fell into a number of categories. To the ones who really wanted to live, he would suggest three things:

1. Get a good doctor. Make sure that you have a great relationship with your doctor. This is your life, and if your physician just treats you as a number or is not prepared to fight alongside you, then make a change.

2. Start to love life. Begin to do the things that would really bring you joy. The impact of experiencing joy and fulfillment in life can activate healing chemicals within the body to aid healing.

3. Join a group. When we share our life experiences with people and feel that we are not alone, then the isolation, loneliness, and pain can be relieved, thus aiding healing.

I guess each of the three suggestions are what we would call common sense; however, when we are diagnosed with an illness, often it's a traumatic experience and it can be difficult to think in this way.

Case Study

I mentioned earlier that my mom had been widowed. It happened twice. When it happened at the age of 53, just when her plans for her future were all in place, the wind was taken out of her sails overnight.

Over the next year, her close friend Anne began to take her for Reiki healing. The healing was great, and Mom really looked forward to her Thursday nights. She would come home after the healing and sit alone, while Anne would go and meet a group of girlfriends. Mom wasn't really a big group person, but gradually she began to go out and have supper with the group. Now the Thursday evenings are her weekly highlight. Recently I heard her talk about one of the girls' anguish about a situation in her life, and I realized that in this big group, Mom's grief had taken on a new perspective—she wasn't the only person in the world who was feeling pain, and the group dynamic has really helped her heal.

I never did join a toddler group when I had Liberty. I didn't want to talk about the trials of motherhood with other young moms—but with hindsight it probably would have been the best thing in the world for me!

Being isolated is a lonely and quite terrifying experience. Could you join a group?

GETTING A HANDLE ON OUR LIVES

When I was 19 years old, I worked in the competitive world of advertising, which was a constant challenge. It was a stressful environment, and I would also put pressure on myself to always be the best in my field.

For about six months, I was feeling under the weather and was having continual outbreaks of thrush, which, as anyone who suffers from it will know, can really wear you down. A young doctor at the time offered me some Valium. I declined the offer and changed doctors that day!

My new doctor asked me about my life, and when he realized that I was stressed out, he suggested TM, or Transcendental Meditation. My husband and I both went to a session, and within a few weeks, my life settled down and I was fine. I was back in control.

I now know that when my blood pressure goes up, or if I get any little illnesses or ailments, I have to look at what is going on in my life, consider my lifestyle, and make changes. Often our lives can be overloaded and stressful . . . maybe the reality is that something might have to give. If there is no space in your life and you feel constantly run down, think about it: Your body is going to react. Medicine isn't always going to be the answer, but a life review may be! So the next time you are ill, take a look at what you are or aren't handling in your life; take some time out to work it all out, and watch your well-being improve.

"Medicine isn't always going to be the answer, but a life review may be!"

Of course in certain circumstances, the power of your mind will not manage to resolve all ills. Genetic conditions and illnesses that have been building over a number of years are often irreversible; however, I feel that we need to do absolutely everything in our power to explore the possibilities of healing.

Once you have done this, then there comes a time to make peace with your condition, stop fighting, and relax if you can. Be as gentle as you can with yourself, and where possible, make the time to do a lot of what you love.

CHAPTER TEN

Making Every Day Special

I know that for many people, the journey of life feels tough.
Every day we hear the international news about disasters in the
world; in the local papers we read about threats in our
communities; we listen to family and friends and hear
of the pain and suffering that those around us are
experiencing. Often we spend huge chunks of time
worrying about the future and what might happen
while we are trying our best to control situations in
our lives that feel impossible to manage; from day to day
we are trying to balance overloaded lives that seem to
overwhelm us. When we aren't worrying about the future, we
are fixated on the past, and the result is that we miss out on
what is happening right under our noses . . . today.

At one time in my life I was working about 18 hours a day and was absolutely exhausted. I didn't spend any real quality time with anyone except the odd friend, and occasionally I'd see my family. I reached my goal at a cost—and that cost was the enjoyment of living life to the fullest each day. By the time I reached my goal, I was tired and worn out with nothing else to give. I believe that if we reach our goals at the expense of losing our enjoyment of life, then we have to seriously ask the question: *What are we doing?* I did, and something had to give! The experience was an invaluable learning curve, and when I compare it with my life today, the comparison is like night and day. I now spend quality time with my daughter; I relax with little Scott, my neighbor who is three; and I spend time having tea and chatting with my elderly neighbors.

My Uncle Malcolm was in the hospital recently. He'd had a bad heart attack and was very ill. Although my schedule was tight, I made an effort to visit him; before, I would never have had—or should I say *made*—the time! I gave him a box of goodies and a card telling him just how I felt about him. He was delighted. We chatted for a long time about the whole question of life and death. The next week he brought me a gorgeous bunch of sweet peas.

In that moment I realized how much richness I had missed out on in the past by not being connected to who and what was important to me. The little bunch of flowers that he picked for me gave me a beautiful, lasting feeling of joy inside, and if I'm honest, it felt even more intense than some of the great feelings of achievement I have experienced in my career. It's amazing how when we really make the effort, and when we invest time in people, the rewards can be so fulfilling. This applies to children, partners, friends, neighbors, creative projects, and gardens, too!

By making time for people, and by appreciating every moment, I feel that I am experiencing a great richness in my life again that I had lost sight of for so long. Outside of business, I am connected to people around me again, and I feel I have reconnected with what is important to me. I haven't given up on setting goals; however, I do feel that I have found a much more manageable balance. You may be thinking that you barely have time to catch your breath right now, so how on earth could you imagine taking time out to connect with people when you have a schedule that doesn't have a spare moment? You may be wondering how on earth you could manage to get your life from where it is right now into a place where you could really enjoy life each day.

It is all a matter of balance. If the scales are firmly tipped in one direction and your life is focused on fear or the future, this part of the book should help you begin to see how you can make some fundamental changes in your daily life. As we've seen, this involves your belief system and thought patterns, and I'm going to help you change the way you think to ensure that your life can move from a daily existence into something that is really worthwhile and fulfilling.

WHAT DOES SUCCESS MEAN TO YOU?

The Oxford Dictionary defines success as: "favorable outcome or accomplishment, attainment of wealth, fame, or position."

In Western society, children are encouraged from a very early age to aim high, achieve, and be successful. Traditionally the education system has not been equipped to recognize and merit the different talents, skills, and individual qualities that each and every human being is born with. I know from my experience in running workshops all over the UK and Ireland that many people have untapped potential and talent. However, their early measures of success have knocked their confidence and ensured that the talent is firmly suppressed by their limiting and fearful beliefs. I hope that if you are one of these people, you will be able to tap in to this potential and play with life a little, as soon as you begin to see yourself as the wonderful, unique person you are!

For so many of us, the emphasis in our school years was about being the best and always striving to do better. In most schools, success and competition was greatly encouraged. This pattern of thinking has been embedded into our subconscious minds so firmly that this is how we measure the way our lives are shaping up.

For many of us, even when we leave school the same thinking pattern prevails. If we don't consider our lives to be a success, then we are often left with feelings of lack, emptiness, poor self-esteem, and low self-confidence. We continue to focus on getting more, being better, or being the best. The expectations of society, our parents, our partners, and our peer groups—not to mention ourselves—

"... I realized how much richness I had missed out on in the past by not being connected to who and what was important to me."

dictate that we should have more money, more possessions, a bigger house, a bigger car, a better education, a better job, and a better partner. Constantly living by these core values, focusing on getting more, and thinking about all the things that we don't have in our lives blocks us from seeing the natural beauty and joy that surrounds us every single day. If this is the belief we are living by, then there are going to be some serious side effects on the journey to succeed.

We may experience feelings of:

• lack—as we feel we have not achieved;
• fear that the world is conspiring against us—especially when we can't get what we want;
• exhaustion—as we constantly struggle to control our life and the people in it;
• emptiness inside—as we constantly strive;
• being numb to others' needs—as we focus firmly on our own goals.

In Eastern wisdom, the foundations for achievement are almost the opposite: Success is about being happy, connected to spirit, fulfilled, calm, energized, and content. How often, on people's deathbeds or at the point of a life-threatening diagnosis, do they talk about regretting—the money they never made, the big car they never bought,

the promotion they never achieved? In these intense and profound moments, when we assess the true value of our lives, the real essence of what is important emerges.

• Think right now: If your life was threatened tomorrow, if you had only 12 months to live, what would be the three things you would most want to do? List them in your journal.
    • Are you going to wait until you find yourself in that position to do what needs to be done?

I truly believe that there needs to be harmony and balance in each and every one of our lives. Of course we need to aspire to create goals in order to fulfill our dreams and aspirations, but our goals and aspirations need to be based on a firm foundation of enjoying our lives. This is a priority if we are to enjoy the journey en route to filling our hearts' desires. There is absolutely no point in striving for future goals if we miss out on the true value and joy of everyday living.

HOW DO WE CHANGE?

So how do we move from worrying about the future and about what we haven't got in our lives to experiencing joy every day? How do we change our feelings of anxiety and stress to peace and calm? Let's take a look at one of the first blocks that we need to address before we work through the principles.

" . . . we need to aspire to create goals in order to fulfill our dreams and aspirations . . . "

WORRYING ABOUT THE FUTURE

So much of our worry and anxiety comes from believing that we need to control every single situation in our lives, and if we can't control the situation or something happens that we don't anticipate, we panic about not being able to deal with the outcomes. Therefore, all our focus and attention and anxiety goes into trying physically and mentally to be in control of every situation we find ourselves in.

When we behave like this we:

• become stressed and anxious;
• focus our minds on outcomes that may never happen;
• exhaust ourselves and negatively affect our health and well-being; and
• focus on the future each and every day and miss out on the joy of today.

When we get into this place, we become frightened, we often feel trapped, our creativity stops flowing, the solutions that could help us are blocked, and it feels like we have nowhere to run. If this feels familiar, then read on— these affirmations and principles can really quiet the storm inside your mind and the tension in your body.

What we need to do when we find ourselves in this situation is to change our focus from the future to the present. Let me show you how to move your negative, frightening, limiting dialogue to that which focuses on love, appreciation, power, and joy—no matter how challenging the situation in your life is. The first step is to remove the block. By understanding these affirmations and practicing them every day, you can truly shift your anxiety habit to one that is much more calm and still. So let's get started.

1. "I always do my best—I release the need to control this situation."

What does this statement mean?

What it means is that you can only do your very best to influence the situation that you are in, and to reduce your anxiety, you must recognize and accept when you cannot influence it anymore. This doesn't mean giving up all hope, it just means that you perhaps need to recognize where the line needs to be drawn in the sand before you continue knocking your head against a brick wall.

The second part of this statement means that you now let go of the need to control the situation. Being in control takes so much energy. When we let go, we stop fighting; often all the tension just melts away the minute we decide to let go. I imagine letting go to be like two people fighting over a ball.

Each has their hands around the ball and they are pulling furiously, trying to get what they want. Often the situation can be seen from a different perspective when we let go. Try it!

How does it make me feel?

When we accept that we are doing our best, we feel a sense of achievement rather than the feelings of lack and emptiness that we get if we do not acknowledge our own efforts.

Acceptance brings a feeling of calm and the realization that you can let go and stop fighting. No longer having to be in control in itself is calming. This challenge can be applied to many different situations—for example, running a business that isn't making money, working at a marriage that has ended, trying to influence a situation with your child, or fighting a lost cause at the office.

"Acceptance brings a feeling of
calm and realization that you can let go
and stop fighting. No longer having to be in
control itself is calming."

Example

A very good friend of mine has a daughter who suffers from drug addiction. The pain that she went through as she tried to influence this situation wore her down tremendously. Each day she would worry about where her daughter was, and she would try to keep her in the house to ensure that she wasn't exposed to the world of drugs. But even when she did so, her daughter found a way to get the drugs. The bottom line was that until her daughter wanted to change and give up drugs, nothing would stop her and she would continue taking them.

As the daughter's life deteriorated, my friend felt her life was suffering, too. One day she said to me, "I am her mother, but I'm just going to have to let go. If I don't, I will be the person in the early grave first." There is no doubt that this was a very painful and difficult decision; however, what she did was the right thing to do. My friend continued to support her daughter as she reached her all-time low; there were days and weeks when she didn't know what she was doing, but when she gave up trying to control the situation, she began to feel that she had a bit of her life back.

2. "I can handle anything that happens to me in my life—I feel calm."

What does this statement mean?

It's amazing how as human beings we can handle so much. In the middle of the night, the phone rings and we hear the devastating news about a loved one who is dying or has a terminal illness. How strong and how resilient we can be, often to our amazement. There are moments when we hear of children who die or are murdered, and we question how we could ever recover from something so dreadful; it is truly incredible how we recover from crisis and tragedy in our lives . . .

I can remember watching my mom struggle for her life when she was widowed for the second time. I remember wondering how on earth she would make it through, and now, two years down the line, she is building up her strength as she begins a new life once again. Mom is a fighter, and even when she hits her lowest ebb, somehow with her courage, strength, and determination, she finds her way back up again.

My dear friend Myra had two miscarriages, and eventually, after a full-term pregnancy, she lost her little baby daughter Amy when she gave birth. She was devastated and so fragile. Again I wondered how she would survive as she closed down all communication with the outside world. Eventually she came back to work and got back on her feet again. One day she took me aside and whispered that she was pregnant again. My heart sank. Once again she had another miscarriage. The hole in her life was enormous, and at the time I wondered how she could ever get back on her feet . . . but she survived! She now has a beautiful little baby girl, Hannah, and she and her husband, Paul, continue to put the pieces of their lives back together again.

In our moments of anxiety and frustration, we believe that we are never going to survive what we are going through; we believe that there is no way through a situation. Have you ever felt these feelings in your life? In retrospect it's amazing how we all survive and find a way. I think if we can learn to rest our minds and train our thoughts to convince ourselves that we can handle whatever happens to us no matter what, we can begin to release feelings of anxiety.

At the same time, I think that we need to accept the limits of what we can do. If you desperately want to deal with something in a better way, in every situation remind yourself that you can only do your very best with the resources that you are equipped with. Then you will always handle the situation to the best of your ability. You can do no more than that. I feel that this will once again bring you peace and ease in your life. So many people panic about the future because they think they won't be able to handle the situations that they are in. We always handle them as best we can and we get through. Worrying about the future never helps.

How does it make me feel?

If we grasp this concept we can experience feelings of great relief and calm. When the panic and the fear subside, we can begin to feel better. Think of the really difficult situations that you have handled before in your life. Perhaps you thought you might not get through something and you did. In what situations could you apply the statement, "I can handle anything that happens to me in my life, I feel calm," in your life right now?

Example

I know of so many people who have been laid off. This announcement often sends us into a blind panic. One day we see ourselves as capable, able, and valuable members of society, then within a moment, our inner gremlins begin to yell at us and our self-doubt comes charging up at great speed. Our image of the future becomes bleak, and we begin to seriously doubt what lies ahead. We often begin to imagine that we will not cope as the responsibilities of daily living and the maintenance of our lifestyle are in serious jeopardy.

Losing a job can be the greatest gift in the world, and depending on how you cope with it, it can either make you or break you. In this situation, remind yourself of the other challenges that you have managed to get through in your life. Being let go doesn't affect your skills, talent, or abilities. Five minutes before being laid off you were the same capable, able, talented person that you were five minutes after you received notice.

When we practice affirmations and remind ourselves that we often need to accept the situations that arise in our lives because they are out of our control, the struggle for control dissolves and we can begin to feel calmer about our lives.

Once we can do this, our next effort has to be to begin to build more joy into our lives. So much joy can come from being grateful for what we do have and making the most of it, rather than striving for what we don't have.

Make a list of 20 things each day that you are grateful for. Choose from things like:

- your child's health;
- your health;
- your ability to pay your bills;
- your car;
- your loving partner;
- your job;
- walks on the beach;
- your time for yourself;
- being shown appreciation at work;
- being appreciated at home;
- your health; and
- being alive.

Make up your own list—look around your home, your family, then your outer world.

This might feel difficult the first few times you try it; however, as you practice refocusing your thoughts, you will begin to see the joy of life opening out in front of you. Even in really tough times, practice this daily, and before you know it, the clouds that hang over you will feel much lighter. Do this exercise for 31 days. Then look back and reflect.

It's amazing how much beauty and joy surround us each day, and sometimes we forget to take the time to notice. There are things in life that can set our spirits free, things that can assault our senses and engage our emotions on a deep spiritual level.

I was at my Body Balance class today at LivingWell Gym just outside Edinburgh. In the class I felt my spirit soar as I did some gentle yoga movements to some powerful music. The music somehow lifted me to a place that nothing else in the world can take me to. Whatever it is for you, I believe it's important that you get a dose of it from time to time—this is the stuff that feeds your soul and spirit, energizes you, and lifts you up onto another level of fulfilment.

What things set your spirit free and allow you to dance with life?

• Walking in a gorgeous green forest
• Watching and listening to a freshwater babbling brook
• Walking by a rushing waterfall
• Walking on a quiet beach
• Working in the heart of nature
• Working with wounded or lost animals
• Listening to inspirational music
• Eating delicious food
• Admiring amazing architecture
• Meditation
• Art
• Doing a creative hobby
• Anything else that makes you feel really alive

Think back to when you were a child. What pursuits made your heart sing? What made you feel energized and refreshed? List what comes up for you in your journal. Then consider how and when you could begin to experience them again.

As adults we live our lives by habit. Doing things we find interesting or exciting can make life feel so much better. In this section we are going to focus on designing an everyday life that will make your heart sing, make you feel fantastic, and that will show you that you're capable of achieving feelings of contentment, fulfillment, happiness, and calm.

Consider the kind of thing that makes getting out of bed in the morning worthwhile. Imagine a day when you looked forward to at least two highlights or two feelings of real satisfaction. They may be as simple as:

- creating a beautiful meal for the family;
- speaking up for yourself;
- planting a pot of herbs;
- sitting by candlelight one evening;
- reading a great novel;
- going for an exhilarating run;
- listening to some wonderful music;
- reading your child a bedtime story;
- having an evening of relaxation in the bath;
- having a coffee at an espresso bar on the way to work;
- designing and planting a garden;
- creating a wonderful new home; or
- anything you can imagine that would work for you.

Whatever it is that makes your heart jump for joy, you need to create a bit of each day.

I love setting goals and achieving them, but I love the way I live my life even more. Every day, my life is a little adventure. I cook different foods, rearrange my furniture to create a new feeling in the house, have special themed evenings and invite friends over, have romantic weekends with my partner, and I go off to secondhand bookshops and clothes stores to see what bargains I can find. I make sure every moment of my day has thought in it, and when I do this it always feels in some way very special.

If I make a new recipe and it flops, I laugh and learn—I love making cakes, and sometimes they appear to have been made by a two-year-old! My daughter is the perfect excuse for having fun baking and cooking. When I cook and the recipe is interesting, Liberty loves to help, and we have a fabulous little time to ourselves. We play Italian opera music while cooking, and eat at the dinner table with a candle in the middle of the table. Sometimes Liberty will pick some wildflowers for the center. Living like this doesn't necessarily take more time, it just takes some planning and imagination. The secret recipe to enjoying life is to have simple little pleasures sprinkled throughout your day and to do lots of different things in your daily life. Break the routines, and when things don't work out quite as planned, that's okay—learn, laugh, and move on.

To create joy in your life, you need to open up your creative thinking. Without creativity, you are left with routine. Creativity, after all, is just a new habit for you to learn. I would like to help you wake up your senses. I want to help you focus on what you have, and help you begin to see it in a new way rather than constantly focusing on what you don't have. To constantly focus on dreams and aspirations and goals that are out of your reach may leave you with feelings of despair, so let's pepper them into your life plan. Let's look at creating joy every day as your priority.

I would like to encourage you to ponder the current shape and feel of your life—what do you do that is the same every day? When did you last do something completely different? When did you travel a different road, eat a completely different breakfast, and smell the shower gel or the soap in the bath and savor the scent? When did you do something different with the kids? When was your last adventure? When did you last feel really sexy? When did you last change your hairstyle or color? When did you last send letters or cards to dear friends or family other than birthdays and Christmas?! When did you last remind yourself of how lucky you are for all the good things in your life? When did you last break out of your routine?

I need you to really question exactly how your life can be different. This is about unlocking your creativity and getting you to question your current routine. When you begin to do things differently and perceive things differently, you can begin to enjoy your every day. On the way you can begin to design plans for the big stuff that you may wish to plan for your future.

THE CREATIVITY JOURNAL

I am now going to introduce you to a technique to get your creative juices flowing. I'm going to help you peel back the onion layers and dream a bit about the way you would love to feel and live in your life. In this exercise I want to tap in to the authentic spirit of who you are; I want to dip into your soul's desires; I want to wake up your senses, your imagination, and your sense of adventure.

We are going to begin to create our foundation for daily living with a creativity journal. This is a scrapbook containing images and phrases that will constantly remind you to dream of the way you would love your everyday life to be. It will give you an opportunity to exercise your imagination to its wildest limits.

How often do you think you would like to do something or say you are going to do something, but you never actually get around to it? How often do you see a picture in a magazine that you think is inspiring, offering you ideas for the way you would love to live your life? How often do you see an image of an interior and think that the next time you design a room you are going to create that look or feel? If we don't

'...dream a bit about the way you would love to feel and live...'

cut the images out, the memory is lost, and chances are that you will forget about the idea forever.

Research proves that if we actually write our goals down, we have more chance of achieving them. It's a bit like writing a list. If we can't remember stuff, we write a list. Task by task we work through the list. When it comes to designing a new life for yourself and perhaps your family, a list is a bit of a weak inspirational attempt; therefore, I am going to share with you my idea to uncover the authenticity of your soul, and unlock your passions and desires for the way you would love your life to be. Once you identify what it is you would really like to do, and how you would like to feel in your life each day, so much more color and texture can be woven into the fabric of your everyday life.

The first time I designed a creativity journal, I was surprised by the collages of images that evolved. I can remember cutting out pictures of the kind of men that I wanted to date: actors, chefs, and gardeners . . . the collage of

faces in front of me was a revelation. At the time I was very single! My socializing habits were pretty limited, and there was a real absence of a relationship in my life. I realized when I cut these images out that I was dating the wrong kind of guy. I was dating businessmen who didn't stimulate me. The collage revealed what I needed to do to attract the type of men I really wanted to meet into my life.

The next thing I noticed as I cut out images for the type of house that I wanted to live in was that there had to be trees everywhere and also lots of windows to connect with the outside world. The Capricorn woman in me needed to be with the earth. The challenge was that my house was by the sea! When you make a creativity journal, it's a reflection of your inner world and the yearnings of your soul; it's a collage of what lights your fire; and if the pictures don't match up with the life that you are living, then it's time to integrate some positive changes into your life.

In Spain I collected lots of magazines to add to the piles I have at home, and within a week or two of arriving back, I sat down to my monthly Sunday ritual of updating and enriching my life plan . . . my creativity journal. Goal charts don't work for me, but somehow the colors, textures, emotion, and inspiration that a creativity journal offers reach the mysterious and untapped realms of my creative spirit. When presented with the colorful inspirational pages of my creativity journal, my subconscious mind drinks up the images and goes to work on creating a plan of how it can help me achieve my wildest dreams. Once you get into the habit of using this tool, your life can be deeply enriched.

CREATING YOUR JOURNAL

There are no hard and fast rules for creating your journal. It's a very personal thing, and it's up to you how you go about it. It can be as random or as ordered as you want it to be. You can choose from the following or create your own headings. You may wish to begin with the first four from this list, or, depending on how thick your scrapbook is, you may wish to have ten sections! Here are some ideas for headings:

- Relaxation time for me
- Romantic relationships
- Health and well-being
- Inspirations for daily work and career
- Creating a home spa
- Fun days for kids
- Dream vacations
- Wonderful weekends away
- Fabulous friends
- Travel and adventure
- Lifelong learning
- Delicious food
- Hobbies and interests
- Inspirational interiors

Vital ingredients to get started:

2 popular magazines that you wouldn't normally buy
2 home-decorating magazines that you really like
2 travel brochures of your dream cruises, vacations, weekend breaks, adventure trips
2 Sunday-supplement magazines
1 glue stick
1 pair of scissors
1 scrapbook that you love the look and feel of

> "Once you get into the habit of using this tool, your life can be deeply enriched."

1 large dose of your favorite drink
1 large pillow/comfy cushion
1 CD of your favorite music
A day to yourself

DIRECTIONS FOR USE

Set aside half a day if you can arrange it. At a later date, you can do this with the kids and with your partner, but it's important to do it on your own to begin with. You need to see a clear picture of who you really are and what you want first.

• Get yourself peaceful and relaxed, unwind, and begin to flip through the magazines and brochures.

Note . . . you may even decide to collect the images over a period of time. Read through magazines at night when you are in bed and a little sleepy and relaxed. Cut the images out and pop them into a lovely basket that you keep at the side of the bed. Place your magazines, colored pens, creativity journal, and so on, in this special place.

• When you see a picture that you like, whether it's a cushion in a color that you would never buy, a look on someone's face that makes you want to feel a certain way, or a scene that you would love to be involved in, cut the picture out. If you see any headlines or slogans that represent a command or an inspirational belief that you would like to adopt, begin to cut out the statements or words.

Note . . . it's important that you don't limit your images and dreams by thinking that you could never have that particular thing. You may find something just like it. Your subconscious will begin to search. Just cut it out, even if you can't imagine how on this earth you can have it.

• Head up the sections that you would like in your journal. You can have as many or as few as you choose. Begin to stick the images into your journal. Pack the pages full of images and words. Avoid leaving white space on the page if you can. Just create a fantastic colorful collage.

• Once completed, leave it on your pillow to read daily and nightly. It's important that you update the journal at least quarterly. Put a message in your calendar. As the seasons change, so will your aspirations and moods. It's important that you update your journal to renew your inspiration and creativity, too!

• Once you have completed your creativity journal, it's important that you put dates for completion of your goals somewhere on the page. You can't leave them in a book as pipe dreams—the real fun begins when you learn to live your dreams.

Once you've created your journal, don't be overwhelmed by the compelling image of the way you would love your life to be if it's very different from the one you are living right now. It's important that you enjoy this as a refocusing tool. So much of what you cut out and paste in will begin to seep into your mind and influence your thoughts . . . especially if you read your journal daily. There will be things in your journal that will perhaps take some really focused attention for you to realize. Please don't put too much pressure on yourself to achieve everything all at once. If you do this you will probably find that you will give up on achieving this way of life after a couple of weeks. Instead, just drink in the images and begin to make some subtle changes—by doing so you will begin to feel very good.

Creativity and creative living is all about imagination. Here are some ideas to stimulate your imagination for everyday creative living.

FRIENDS:
SAMPLING FOR FREE

One Saturday afternoon, dress up and head off to a department store. Ask the girls at the beauty counters for some samples of their face and body products to try out at home. Make it your mission to collect as many free samples as possible for your "pamper" evening. Make the time and have a wonderful bath with a glass of chilled wine. Light some candles and then try out some of your samples—experiment with new makeup, and try doing your hair a completely new way. Change the color if you like! Then watch a movie or read a novel. You could do this with a friend. It's a great new way to experiment with new products for your skin and your face. I remember I did this as a teenager—why stop as an adult? It's fun!

FAMILIES:
AN ENERGIZING WALK TOGETHER

Imagine taking a brisk walk in the forest with the family, everyone all bundled up. You might even want to take a flask of tea to enjoy in the open air! Everyone could collect some blackberries and wildflowers and upon returning home, the kids could make a blackberry pie—who cares how it turns out, it's homemade and the fun is in experimenting. When you serve the pie on the table, place it next to the flowers and light a candle. Munch the dessert while watching a family movie!

This mini-adventure gets you out in the fresh air, exercising, and using your imagination and your creativity—and it's also about savoring the moment and enjoying the fruits of your labor with the most precious people in your life. That's what living is about.

TRAVEL:
MAKING TRAVEL AN ADVENTURE

You may decide that you would like to travel to a country you have always dreamed of going to. To begin moving toward your goal you could start to collect prices and details from travel agents. You could also search the Web for all the information you can find on the place before you visit. You could take an afternoon out, go to a bookstore, and treat yourself to coffee as you leisurely browse in the travel sections. Read the *Lonely Planet* guides and learn all about the traditions, cultures, food, entertainment, and accommodation reviews. All of this can be done on a pretty low budget, and it's a highly enjoyable experience on the way to your goal!

In this part of the book, we are going to look at how you can begin to design a new way of living, where you can savor special moments, and where you can begin to play and have fun again! I feel that so often when we talk about goals we just think of hard work; the word itself conjures up failed New Year's resolutions, diets that haven't worked, or exercise regimes that have failed. I often think of a goal as a high-pressure corporate term used as a mechanism to manipulate and drive people to achieve huge sales targets and material aspirations.

This weekend, or the next time you have the opportunity, create half a day to begin to compile your creativity journal. Begin to create your design for living.

Good luck! This is just the beginning.

Dawn Breslin Creativity Journal

CHAPTER ELEVEN

The Big Stuff

The stuff that dreams are made of!

We are now going to explore the BIG STUFF, the aspirations and dreams that lie like nuggets of gold in your soul and spirit, unexplored and untapped. These nuggets are like the innermost layers of the onion. They are what we imagine would make a huge difference in our lives.

These dreams and aspirations are the key to a life that you would find stimulating and exciting. They come in all different shapes and sizes: going back to college to study, changing your career, getting a new relationship, getting into shape, or buying the car or the house of your dreams. They may be material goals or they may be the opposite. Maybe the dream is to abandon the career and have a life with the kids, or you may want to leave corporate life and become a ski instructor. Whatever it is for you, the principles in this section will apply if you would like to achieve a goal.

I am a little wary of goals, as my absolute belief is that daily life and appreciation are so much more important than achieving goals—however, as a compulsive goal-setter, I must admit that if you are living life to the fullest and you don't compromise your daily life too much, achieving goals is one of the most fantastic feelings in the world. I have always set goals and enjoyed the rewards of achievement, whether it is financial or emotional. But please do be aware that there *must* be a balance between your future focus and your daily design for living!

Having said that, I have always been excited about goal-setting, initially for myself, and then later as I began to help other people see a clear path toward their own dreams and aspirations. What I found addictive was when I heard someone speak with passion about a business idea that they had held in their heart for years, but had never gotten around to making a reality. I so wanted to help them. People would talk to me about the jobs that were eating up their lives, and their burning desire to spend more time with the kids. I'd hear people talk about their dreams of traveling around the world, but I'd watch them stay stuck in whatever place they lived.

I would often hear the sounds of people's hearts bursting with emotion, their minds overflowing with creativity about all the things that would give them wings and offer them so much joy, fulfillment, and happiness in their lives. I knew that they had no real plans or direction in place to achieve these dreams or aspirations.

Most of the time when people are sharing their dreams with me, I find that they talk about making things happen. However, the little gremlin inside their heads keeps reminding them that there is no way they can actually achieve their goal right now ... maybe one day in the future they'll get around to it. In my heart I feel frustrated and all I want to do is help get them there.

My passion became an obsession, and in 1999 I had to make the move to achieve my burning desire and set up my own training company. I rented office space in a little business center and rented a desk that was sandwiched between Fella, a gorgeous entrepreneurial guy who was a whiz on the computer, and an outrageous interior designer called Anne Hunter. Between the three of us, we sorted out our computer challenges and over a cup of tea we would boost each other's confidence to succeed. It was a fantastic little start to building the business I run today.

In the beginning I was scared and nervous: I'd never trained before, I'd never worked on my own computer, and I'd never had to pay my own wages. I did have a burning desire to do it, I was excited about the future, and, like an Olympic athlete, although I had butterflies in my tummy, I knew exactly where I was going and couldn't wait to get started. I can still remember vividly my first ever training experience. My dear friend Jon McLeod offered me my first break. He paid me $900 to deliver a three-hour session on goal-setting to a select group of his team. I was so nervous, I couldn't stay out of the bathroom!

In that session I delivered exactly what we are going to explore in this part of the book. Three weeks after my session, I had the feedback, and the results were wonderful: Someone had given up smoking; someone who was gay had come out; someone who wanted a promotion approached the boss and worked toward it; people were buying new cars, new apartments, and all sorts of things. Someone even resigned! Within one year I had trained Jon's whole team at all of his branches, and the results were fantastic.

After my training sessions, Jon implemented goal charts for which the team would cut out images of their goals and aspirations and paste them up on the wall at work. At each weekly appraisal, as part of his management strategy, Jon would work with them to help them achieve their goals. His commitment was huge and the results staggering.

From that first day, things got easier. I realized that this obsession and passion that I had in my heart could actually be communicated and implemented into people's lives. This convinced me that I was on the right track in achieving my very own goal of helping people take control and make positive changes in their lives. I was now convinced that I could do this—it really worked and nothing could stop me now!

THE LUCK FACTOR

The journey has been tough to get to where I am today. TV work, authoring books, and writing for magazines and newspapers doesn't come easily. You have to prove your worth first, and you have to have a story to tell. I can remember wondering when I was younger if anyone would ever discover me. I so wanted to be an actress, but I wasn't doing anything about it. How would anyone know that this was my dream?! Now I know that being discovered is something that generally happens only in the movies. For 99 percent of the population to get to where we really want to go, it takes hard work. So if you think that you don't need goals, and you don't need to be focused because something miraculous is going to happen to you and your life might just take a great turn without effort—think again!

There is a brilliant book called *The Luck Factor* by Robert Wiseman, a scientist who has dedicated a chunk of his life to exploring, through university research and scientific trials, how luck is not something that comes out of the blue. The maxim "We create our own luck" is ultimately the key to how we go about cultivating luck and good fortune. Even the unluckiest of us can change our luck by changing the way we think. In *The Luck Factor*, Wiseman shows that building or inheriting brilliant habits of strong positive belief in every situation in pursuit of a goal is the most direct way to achieving any kind of success in life. I guess if we were really to determine who is lucky and who isn't, people who have positive belief will always get a head start. If by nature you always see the dark, negative, or cynical side of life or life experience, then you stand less chance of formulating your own good luck. This doesn't mean you can't have it, it just means that you will have to work twice as hard to attract it.

Some people believe in the notion of being "born lucky." This book shows that the only thing that's certain about luck is that the people who experience a lot of it have an unfaltering belief in whatever it is they are pursuing.

HOW WE ARE SHAPED ON OUR JOURNEY

The journey to our goals plays an important part in what shapes us. I feel that each time I have taken a knock, I've gotten up off my knees, dusted myself off, and learned a valid lesson. Sometimes I've wished I'd learned the lessons more quickly, but I guess that's just human nature, and I don't bash myself too hard for not being perfect anymore!

On my journey of life, I've skinned my knees and bruised my heart, I've felt sick with nerves, and I've cried with fear; however, one thing never faltered—without fail I continued to see my goal clearly and never once lost faith. Five years ago I remember sitting on the wall at the bottom of my garden with my friend Mhairi. It was an autumn night and I'd just bought an old two-bedroom house that was overrun with rats! Sitting on the wall seemed like a great alternative to being in the house, as it was in an uproar from the renovation!

I remember talking about the first workshop I wanted to run, discussing the details of my book, and talking about when I would work in TV. At that time it was all a pipe dream, but I could see it all clearly in my mind, and as I shared my ideas with supportive friends and family, I just knew in my soul it was all going to work out—if I put the hard work in. Mhairi never doubted me—she was exactly the type of friend you need when you have a dream. She supported me the whole way, even on the tough days!

I put the effort in, and believe me—it was tough. I remember turning up at my mother's house some nights after work and Mom, concerned for my well-being, thought I was working too hard and that I needed to take a break. The business had eaten up all my money, so I needed to keep going, and I really believe an angel or someone up above was looking after me because there were times when I don't know how I got through. One thing that remained constant through the whole experience was my unfaltering focus on the goal. I had worked so hard and nothing was going to stop me from getting where I wanted to go.

Here I am now, living my dream, almost five years later. I feel I have changed as a woman, I have changed as a mother, and I have probably changed as a partner, a friend, and a daughter. I am stronger and have been molded by facing up to some tough life experiences. Running a business can have a great impact on your personal and professional relationships. The trial of learning from experience no doubt will continue until I am old and gray. Going for what you really want in your life can change you; the tough times shape your character, make you more robust, and more resilient, force you into a corner sometimes, and teach you how to deal with things you never thought you could deal with.

In this way, life's rich array of lessons can become your everyday experience. You are often faced with a choice—you can lie down and let life take you and knock you or you can stand back up, take what you need to from the experience, learn, and grow. Sometimes we need a little time to recover, but staying down hurts more! Realizing our dreams, touching the stars, feeling a sense of achievement, and making a difference in our and other people's lives are some of the most fulfilling experiences in the world, and in this section I am going to teach you the key principles to goal-setting that I have followed to get me where I am today.

Whether your goal is making a definite difference in the way that you feel about yourself, taking some really good quality time to recharge your batteries, or even if it's about buying a nifty little sports car or a fabulous house in the country, the principles outlined in this section are universal and apply to any goal big or small.

ARE YOU A RUDDERLESS SHIP BOBBING ABOUT WITH NO DIRECTION?

Where are you going in your life right now? What flickers of inspiration have you stumbled across as you have read through this book? Think about some of these questions. What type of relationship would you love to have with your partner? If you are single, in your heart of hearts, would you really love to meet someone special? What would you love to do for work every day, and what type of people would you like to have in your life?

What sort of interests would you like to pursue? What would you like your body to look like? If you don't know the answers to these questions, chances are that you are either very happy with your life right now and you don't need to ask the questions, or most likely, as you have bought or been given this book as a gift, your answer may be, "I don't really know what I want." If you don't know what you want out of life, then what you will get out of life won't be very much.

Do you feel like you are hovering, bobbing up and down on the waves like a boat without a direction? Or do you feel like you are going round and round in circles? You might even feel dizzy as you churn ideas around in your head about what you could do with your life day after day! If you aren't putting any effort into the relationship, the chances are that it may be dull and boring; that is, of course, unless your partner is doing all the work, in which case, one day he or she might get tired of it and stray!

If you don't really care about your job, you might spend most of the time being bored and uninterested in the workplace, where you spend most of your waking hours! When you are uninterested, you don't perform particularly well and then you begin to feel that you're stuck in a rut: You need the money but hate the job. It's too much hassle to leave, so you'll just stay for another year or two until something really good comes up. Are you looking for something new, or could the place you are in become better if you just change the way you look at it?

If you don't look after your body by respecting it, relaxing it, feeding it nourishing foods, and exercising, it won't look or perform the way you want it to. Your mental and physical well-being are the cornerstones of your life. If you feel bad each day emotionally or physically, this can have a huge impact on your health and well-being. On a cosmetic level, the perfect body doesn't just arrive with a sprinkle of fairy dust—as I know. While I'm writing this book, I'm preparing my body for a television show on Discovery Health, and losing 16 pounds is no easy task! It requires discipline, focus, and determination—otherwise my chin, upper arms, and middle-aged midsection will all show up in glorious technicolor, and via the unforgiving nature of TV, the fat is automatically multiplied by two!

So what do you really need to focus on in your life right now? What really needs atten-tion? If the answer is "Everything," then chances are that you feel pretty stuck right now. So let's look at creating some focus and direction in the areas where you need it most. If, on the other hand, you have loads of goals but absolutely no time and you just crave time out for you, or you need relaxation, then we have to look at reducing the amount of goals and creating some strong personal boundaries to ensure that we recharge your batteries. We need to unleash your cre-ativity to work out a creative plan to get you on the road to where you really want to go.

DO YOU REALLY NEED A NEW GOAL?

Just before we delve into the world of refo-cusing our lives, it is important to remember how a renewed outlook on a stifling situation is often all that we need to address rather than jumping in and making great changes we might regret later on.

I remember my first experience in the field of personal development. My automatic reaction was that I wanted to change absolutely every-thing in my life, because for the first time in

"I was the only person stopping me from doing whatever I wanted to do."

years I realized that I was the only person stopping me from doing whatever I wanted to do and that I could change whatever I wanted, whenever I wanted. I feel that a little warning can be helpful at times like this: When our enthusiasm goes through the roof, we can often find ourselves acting hastily. My advice now would be: Give everything a really good final attempt to make it better before you make any drastic life changes.

ENDING A MARRIAGE OR RELATIONSHIP

Many people believe that they are trapped by their partners and that's why they can't do what they want to do. I find that in reality, people have set up their own self-limiting habits and beliefs that keep them from moving forward in their lives. Somehow, over time, they begin to blame their partners for the fact that they aren't living their lives the way they want to, when actually the limits have absolutely nothing to do with their partners.

There is no doubt, if you understand the principles of this book, that if you refocus your goals, your partner is going to notice a big difference in you. Wouldn't you if the roles were reversed? Think about this.

Like any new habit, people take time to adjust. Give your partner, your boss, your friends, and your parents the opportunity to accept your new way of thinking—you might be surprised by the end result. I've heard of marriages blossoming once the dust settles and couples start working on this stuff together.

Please be clear that I am not saying, "Don't make changes." In situations where people are being mentally and physically abused, I would recommend that someone should definitely get out of the relationship with the partner, parent, boss, or relative. If this is not the case, I suggest that before you act hastily, just give it your best shot. If that doesn't work over a period of time, then you can make your decisions knowing that you did everything you could.

CHANGE OF JOB/BOSS

With the right attitude, we can begin to enjoy the things in life that we often detest. When we make a decision that we hate something or someone, we often carry that thought with us all the time and don't stop to review it. I'm suggesting that if we look at a situation differently, if we take our focus off all the negative things about something or someone and remind ourselves of what's good about the situation or the person, we might find that the person or the situation isn't so bad after all.

So many people complain to me about their jobs, yet when I listen to them I realize that they love the environment, the team-work, and the community aspect of their position. When we become disgruntled about one par-ticular aspect, it can cloud the whole situation. Think about it—in your life, what do you complain about that really isn't so bad?

Once we shift gears and begin to view the sit-uation from a different perspective and decide to really make an effort, things can change dramatically in our lives. Some people believe that to change a situation completely is the only way to feel better. The reality is that when we change our way of viewing something and see it from a different angle, the upheaval of change can sometimes be avoided. Think this one through before being too hasty!

REACH FOR THE STARS

My oldest friend, Lindsay, always says that even if I told her I was going to the moon for dinner on Friday night, she would believe me. She knows that I have come to a point in my life where whatever I tell her I'm going to do, she knows I'll do it! I use the principles in this book, and I am in a place right now where no challenge is too great.

So many people keep the doors to their fantastic futures firmly closed. The benchmark for the way they live their lives is determined by:

• what their families have achieved in the past;
• what their immediate social environment dictates;
• what their current income is, not what they could potentially earn if they were to make some changes to their work life;
• only doing things that have been done by others and have been tested first; and
• doing what is familiar to them.

No real pleasurable, fulfilling goal can be culti-vated with this state of mind. Whether you come from a mining village, whether you are paid the minimum wage for
your day job, whether

you have five children and no cash in the bank, your mind is capable of taking you into a realm of possibility where you can dream of the life you would love to live. Your life can be so different from the one you are living today. You might not know how on earth you are going to get to these dreams, but the first and most important step in the world is actually opening the door to the possibility that things can be so different.

Narrow vision leaves so many people in a place where they feel that their potential is untapped; they feel unfulfilled and caught up on the treadmill of life. Here is an example of someone who kept the doors to her future securely closed.

Case Study

I remember doing a workshop for unemployed people in a an equal-opportunity group. The session was jam-packed, and at the end I held up my creativity journal to show the goal-setting section. My creativity journal was crammed with all of my goals big and small. As I flipped through the pages of the book, I held up an image of a beautiful, high-quality kitchen that I loved. As I showed it to the group, a lady in the front row said, "I would never put that in my book, because there is no chance of my having anything like that." The truth of the matter was that at that point in my life, there was no way that *I* could afford a gorgeous designer kitchen; however, I was never going to block my dreams and think that I couldn't ever have something like it. The reality of the situation is that the picture inspired me to have a similar style of kitchen from a store that was much less expensive.

The point that I'm making here is that even if you can't have the original, then you can work toward having something like it. If you believe there is a possibility of moving toward the original goal, make sure you give it your best shot. I believe by putting these aspirations into our creativity journal, we will always move in a positive direction in our lives. Just make sure again that the desire for the goal doesn't compromise the magic of your everyday living. How many things have you just written off in your life by uttering the words "I can't have anything like that"? Stop here and just think for a moment about how those words close the door to so many opportunities in your life.

Earlier in the book we talked about ways to unlock the creativity that hasn't been exercised for years. You may not have been in the habit of daydreaming about how your life could be; you may be in the habit of writing ideas off before you even explore the possibility of achieving them. We looked at the common blocks and habits when we contemplate achieving new goals, such as lack of confidence, lack of money, lack of time, and lack of creative thinking. How would you like to shop from this wish list?

Would you love to be invited to a party or to a bonfire on a beach? Would you love to receive a beautiful letter from a friend or family member telling all the wonderful things they think of you? Would you love to go fishing on a lake with a sack lunch for some total peace and tranquillity? Would you love someone to give you the time to create some relaxation in your life? Would you love someone to take your stress away? Would you love to be taken to a country that you have always dreamed of visiting? Would you love to be taken on a romantic weekend with your partner in Paris? Would you love someone to promote you because they can see your talent? Would you love all your difficult situations at work or home to be solved without having to deal with them? Would you love someone to encourage you to set up your own company or study something you love? Would you love to create a home that feels like the ones you see in magazines? Would you love to be slim, with a different hairstyle and new makeup? Would you love to meet the person of your dreams? Would you love to have a little fluffy kitten?

Wishes don't generally come true without hard work . . .

Here's the truth . . . you can have all of this stuff if you make the effort and focus your mind on your goal. It's all there for you, and with a little bit of hard work, you can begin to carve these types of ideals into your life. It may not be that someone else is going to do all these things for you; however, if you really aspire to any of these dreamy aspirations and you are prepared to work hard at the principles I am teaching in this section, you too can have so much more.

Wishes on the whole don't happen on their own—follow the principles in this section and watch how something you regarded as a pipe dream may come true!

Earlier we looked at unlocking your creativity and keeping a record of your life goals. In my creativity journal I have images of Courtney Cox's house in Hollywood, Range Rover cars, the ultimate life balance, wedding bells, and more little people in my life! As my journals have evolved over the years, so have my dreams and aspirations. The images are

"By putting these aspirations into our creativity journal, we will always move in a positive direction in our lives."

perfect for creating food for my imagination. They fuel my subconscious mind and motivate me to move toward my dreams daily.

The influence of the images and the seeds of thought that these pictures have created won't go away—I'm still working toward images I cut out five years ago! So please be gentle with yourself. Start with creating a goal for something like "me time," feel the positive effects of achieving satisfaction in this area of your life, and then move on to something else. Don't go out and try to build Rome in a day. If you take on too much all at once, you will experience deep feelings of despair. Be gentle with yourself, and take one goal at a time. So let's get started with the principles for actually achieving your goals.

Wanting the Goal with a Passion

PRINCIPLE NUMBER ONE

Setting a goal is like directing a bright searchlight onto the image of your dream. It's about imagining every detail of that dream and seeing it in your mind's eye like a glorious technicolor vision seen through a huge magnifying glass. It's about creating a compelling vision of something you want so badly that you feel compelled to chase after it with all of your heart and soul.

The first principle is that you must desire the goal. I can remember my friend Michael saying to me, "I don't know how I do it. I'm always broke, yet everything I put my mind to, everything I really want to do badly, I always seem to find the money to do it." He wasn't sure how it worked, but it seemed that he always just managed to scrape by. Right now he's working as a volunteer with children in Tibet—he's been there for the past four years. I think Michael's life, like many other people I know, is filled with passion and enthusiasm. It would appear to me that if you have passion and enthusiasm and you really want something enough, you will always find a way to achieve your goal.

So the first principle of achieving any goal is to want it badly enough. If you don't really care about achieving the goal, you will never achieve it. That may sound simplistic, but it's true.

On a scale of one to ten how much do you want to do the following?

- Add sparkle to your relationship
- Find a new relationship
- Find a new job
- Change the way you feel about your job
- Set up your own business
- Improve your physical body
- Improve your confidence
- Improve the way you feel
- Rediscover the sparkle in life

If your answers don't score ten out of ten, then we have to question whether you really want change, or whether you are actually happy the way you are. Once you have asked yourself these questions and scored your results, ask yourself this: If right now I told you that making this decision would be the one you would take to your deathbed with you, how would you feel? It's a tough one. However, if you don't look at making changes right now, when will you do it?

I reckon that if you don't set a timetable for reassessing these questions about your life, then the chances are that nothing will change. You will just spend your life on wishful thinking. If that's the case, revert to the Design for Life section (Chapters 7 and 8), put your focus and attention there, and stop beating yourself up for never achieving anything. I'm sorry if you feel that I'm being tough on you—I'm just trying to talk you through this and make sure that you are not procrastinating because of fear, old thinking patterns, and your ingrained

habits, which can stop you from doing the things that you would really love.

Once you have worked through those questions, I would like you to consider this: To increase your motivation and desire for this goal, what could you do? Let me give you some examples.

LOSING WEIGHT
Put photos of yourself when you feel you looked good onto your mirror or on the fridge. Hang a pair of pants that you would love to fit into in a place where you can see them every day.

TAKING A COLLEGE COURSE
You could phone a college for a syllabus and perhaps have a chat with one of the professors or lecturers. Once you begin to talk this through, you will feel the adrenaline running through your veins, and this will inspire you on to the next step.

NEW HOME BY THE SEA
You could visit some houses for sale that have views of the sea and get the feeling of how it would be to live there. Your subconscious would get so excited that it would want be on the constant lookout for opportunities!

DRIVE A SPORTS CAR

Stick a picture up on your fridge, and if that doesn't excite you, you could test-drive the car that you love. Feel the motivation levels go through the roof once you have done this.

I test-drove a sports car after not believing I deserved one. I lived in a gorgeous house by the sea after visiting an area where there was no way that I could afford a home. When we really want something badly enough, we will do everything in our power to achieve it. I lived in an area where the houses were out of my budget; however, I compromised and bought a house that was in need of total refurbishment to achieve my dream of over-looking the sea. It took time to create a won-derful home, and over three years I trans-formed the house.

When I test-drove the car with Liberty, it felt like Thelma and Little Louise! I wanted the car so much. The saleswoman told me the price was $36,000. I couldn't imagine how I could ever afford to spend that kind of money on a car. I always believed cars should be bought outright, as that was the belief of my father. The saleswoman advised me that I could have the car for $530 per month. I still couldn't imagine how I could manage to afford that price. I wanted the car so much that when I went for my new job interview, I made it a condition of acceptance that I should have a car allowance rather than opt into the company car program. The company agreed, and within three weeks of viewing the car of my dreams, I was driving it! Creative thinking went a long way!

EXERCISE

In your journal, list three goals that you would really love to achieve. Once you have done so, test the level of desire by scoring your goals on a scale of one to ten. If the desire does not reach seven, what measures could you take to build the desire to achieve this goal?

" ... over three years I transformed the house ... "

Believe in Your Dream

PRINCIPLE NUMBER TWO

To ensure that you achieve your goal, your conviction and sense of belief should almost be cast in stone. I'm not suggesting that it won't wobble from time to time, because everyone's belief suffers from the wobble factor occasionally. At the very conception of your goal, however, if you don't actually believe with your heart and soul that you can achieve it, then you probably *won't* achieve it. If you suffer from self-doubt, it will run rampant in your mind, impacting your actions, and it will ultimately sabotage any possibility of your reaching your goal.

In the section on affirmations, we worked hard on creating powerful internal and external dialogue. This will be absolutely essential to enable you to reach your goal. It is so important that you feel 100 percent confident about aiming in the direction that you are going. You must believe in your own talents and abilities to ensure that you have the courage, drive, and determination to achieve the goal. It's amazing how creative thinking can take hold when we want something passionately.

We must be aware of the belief trap: We think we have mastered our belief system only to find yet another thought or belief that is blocking our clear pathway to our dream. The best way to check out how focused your belief is, is to ask yourself honestly: *Do I believe that I can really achieve this goal?* On a scale of one to ten, assess your answers. If your scores are less than seven, question why you are not scoring ten. What do you believe or fear is holding you back? Once you work through this and manage to get your score up to ten by either questioning your fears or doing some new affirmations, then you will be ready to take on the goal.

The odd thing about unfaltering belief and hope in a dream is that there is often a power that accompanies belief. It's a little like a prayer, in that if we want something so badly and focus so hard on what we really want, and if we are doing everything in our power to attract the goal, then things almost mysteriously begin to come our way and fall into place.

I believe that when I want something badly, if that desire is for the greater good, then I feel that I am guided toward it. I have a feeling that I am not alone and am working together with some higher force that guides me toward my goals—especially the ones that are geared toward helping people.

People who pray often experience the same thing. Have you ever wanted something so much that you have focused and focused on it, and almost mysteriously it comes your way? There are many huge and complex metaphysical and scientific explanations for the theories of attracting what we want into our lives through the power of belief; however, now is not the time to go into it—I'll save that for another book!

Visualize Every Detail of Your Dream

PRINCIPLE NUMBER THREE

The power of visualization is an incredible tool. To see your outcomes in your mind's eye before they actually come into your reality strengthens the impact of the desire, and the belief that you can actually achieve your desired outcome.

Again, if you struggle to visualize the outcome of your goal in your mind's eye, then perhaps you can't actually imagine achieving your goal. Visualization is a bit like daydreaming. Imagine you are decorating a room in a house: As you choose the fabrics and wallpapers, you begin to create a picture in your mind of the final effect of the whole room. Visualization for goals works in exactly the same way. The creativity journal is a creative visualization aid, but to bring all your ideas in the journal to life, you really need to imagine every single tiny detail of your goal in your mind's eye. When we do this, we feed these positive, encouraging images and thoughts to our brain and our subconscious mind. When the brain receives these images, it begins to increase the desire for the goal and in turn strengthens your belief that you can achieve it.

EXERCISE

Each morning before you begin your day, take five minutes as you lie in bed to run the picture of your desired goals over and over in your mind. See the faces of the people around you, feel the feelings that you would love to feel, imagine the sounds and the smells of everything in your desired scenario. Enhance the colors in your image to make it more realistic, increase the sounds of the atmosphere that surrounds you. If your image is a little hazy, adjust the focus of your visualization. Make this a daily ritual.

Each night as I flip through my creativity journal, I gaze into the images on the pages, and within seconds I'm almost in a trancelike state as my imagination takes flight and I begin to see myself inside the goal. All of the detail is in front of me in glorious technicolor. I imagine the scenarios of the reality in my mind, and my dream unfolds in front of me. I am there inside the image that I'm looking at in my book. My imagination really feels like my reality. This state feeds my subconscious mind, allowing me to confidently believe that everything is achievable.

Expect the Dream to Come True

PRINCIPLE NUMBER FOUR

What I mean by expectation is that one must actually expect the outcome of the goal to happen without any doubt at all. To expect the outcome to be achieved, we must speak as if the goal is in progress. This often involves affirming something that in reality hasn't actually been achieved yet. Let me give you an example.

Someone who really wants to set up their own company may be doing affirmations every day. They may be affirming that they are now in the process of running their own ceramics company, when in reality they are still employed full-time in their current job at the bank. By implementing the principle of expectation, they will begin to talk to people as if they are already experiencing the success of their desired goal. So the person who wants to open up the ceramics company will switch from talking about their current job at family or social gatherings, and in turn they will begin to talk about the ceramics business that they are in the process of setting up. What you are doing here is creating:

• an expectation of yourself that will put pressure on you to achieve the goal more quickly; and

• an expectation of yourself to prospective clients and business associates; by "being open for business" you open the door for demand to begin.

When you do this, people will begin to ask you when you will be open for business so you can begin to generate your desired outcome more quickly. People often talk of the coincidences that arise when they start to connect with people associated with their desired outcomes. I feel that there is no such thing as coincidence. I believe that because you are actually unlocking your dream from your mind or your heart and letting the reality of your ideals connect with other people, opportunities are going to arise naturally.

So talk about your goals as if they are already happening. This may feel a bit scary at first, but you will be amazed at how quickly things begin to come to you when you start to express to others what you are trying to achieve. Who can you begin to share your goals with? Think of two or three people that you can mention your goals to this week. Talk as if they are happening now. You will be surprised by how good this feels.

Do Something about the Goal Today

PRINCIPLE NUMBER FIVE

Here we go, truth time again. You can sit in a corner all your life, believing that something great will happen to you. You can believe that you are talented beyond belief. You can believe you are the best thing since sliced bread, but the awful truth is that nothing is ever going to happen to you unless you do something about your dream or aspiration. When we take action, it has an incredible momentum. Action brings

responses in waves, and when we begin to do something about our dream—when we talk about it, make the phone calls and do what we really need to do—momentum can be like a domino effect. Before you know it, life can really feel completely different and quite fantastic.

The world, the country, your parents, and your partner don't owe you a living, and the sooner you accept this, the better equipped you will be to turn your own beliefs and desires into real-life experiences. So often I have seen absolutely brilliant talent go to waste because of a lack of effort, and this is such a shame. I have many musician friends, and when I ask them what they would like to do with their talent, they tell me lovely long stories about their dreamy ambitions. They believe that one day a talent scout will spot them and their lives will be rosy. Ten years down the line, many of them have never been discovered. Week by week they practice, and they say that they have sent a couple of demos of their work off to DJs. When they get no response, they give up.

We need to understand this lesson. Life is like a hurdle race. So often on the way to our dreams and aspirations we are going to fall. It's inevitable, so be ready for it. You may do something and get no response. I've been there, and yes, it is demoralizing, but if we do not learn from our lessons and charge on regardless, our dreams could slip like fine white sand between our fingers. Unless we learn quickly and take action, we may as well forget the goal. People believe that one day, something magical will happen to them; one day, everything in their lives will be different. I need you to really think about this statement. If you are waiting for life to happen to you ... GET REAL NOW! This just doesn't happen. Sheer hard work and determination gets you to where you want to be, and the sooner you face up to it, the closer you will be to living your dreams.

I have read many times that 90 percent of a person's success has been attributed to sweat and hard work, and the remaining 10 percent may be about being in the right place at the right time.

Ask yourself this. What do you need to do today to make some real movement toward your goals? What do you need to add to your list of things to do tomorrow that may take you in the direction of the kind of life you really want to live?

"If you are waiting for life to happen to you ... GET REAL NOW! This just doesn't happen. Sheer hard work and determination get you to where you want to be, and the sooner you face up to it, the closer you will be to living your dreams."

PART II

Dealing with the Tough Stuff—
Healing a Bruised Soul

CHAPTER TWELVE

Creating Some
Powerful Foundations

When you feel strong and confident, you can make the changes that you need to make in life to swim with the tide, not against it. Like a hot-air balloon, your heart can take flight if you address letting go of the baggage that you have accumulated over the years. In this part of the book, I will help you create an anchor in your soul to make you feel strong again.

There are some key techniques that I believe you should master before moving on to any affirmation or goal-setting routine. It's important to build your self-esteem and self-confidence to make you strong, and you need to ensure that your found-ations are firmly embedded so that when you have to face the challenges that change invariably brings, you will have a well-established supportive dialogue woven into your external and internal vocabulary.

My advice to anyone embarking upon life changes would be to ensure that you have the key principles of loving and respecting yourself firmly in place before you begin your affirmation routine or goal-setting plan. Making changes can often be tough. Leaving a difficult relationship, speaking up to an aggressive boss, or not allowing anyone to walk over you all take courage and inner strength. Here we are going to secure the foundations of your self-beliefs and teach you some positive new habits before we get started on the big stuff.

I would suggest that you read this section intently and question yourself honestly. It would be so easy to skim through this material and do nothing with it.

The next challenge will be to record what you feel in your journal and then begin to implement the exercises into your everyday life.

Be really gentle with yourself here; what you are trying to do is challenging. You are dealing with the tough stuff, and it can take a bit of time before you begin to see the effects. Read through the case studies. I know that this material really can work, because I have seen the results so many times.

If you feel you are working at it and it's not happening for you, take a break for a few weeks and then come back and try again. Sometimes the will is there, but for whatever reasons the affirmations and exercises just aren't working for you at this time. That's okay. For some people it can take three to six months before they feel any impact or benefit. Just remember that it's taken you a lifetime to get to where you are now, so give yourself a chance to let it all cook slowly.

Remember the analogy of the diet. Just by eating the right food we don't necessarily lose weight overnight. Sometimes it takes a little perseverance to feel the change. If you struggle at first, that's okay. Come back again and give it another try.

If you find after doing these exercises that they really aren't working, please seek some help from a trained professional. This is life-changing work that can really set you free, and if you don't make the effort to spend time on it right now, where are you going to be in five years' time?

Each and every one of these internal and external challenges can trap people for lifetimes. It may sound a bit flippant of me to say that they are just ingrained habits that need to be changed or reframed. However, this is the truth, and if you can manage to turn the thoughts or behavior around, your life can take a massive leap forward. The best you can do is commit to this and give it your very best shot. Here we go . . .

MAKING A COMMITMENT

Until you commit 100 percent to making changes in your life, this book won't work for you. But if you read it intently and practice the exercises daily, you can take a huge step forward in your life.

Sometimes when we have been knocked around by life, it's really tough to get back up on our feet again or to recover from what has happened. As a result of the experience, we may have taken a bit of a blow to our self-esteem or self-confidence; we may be holding on to anger and bitterness from the past, or we may be feeling guilty about something that we either have or haven't done. Regardless of what has affected you, chances are that these emotions have an impact on your relationships with others and may cloud your vision of the future.

Our bruised souls can't be seen by the human eye. They aren't as obvious as physical abuse, divorce, illness, or disability. Sometimes a dominant parent, peer, or boss may have affected our lives. Maybe we've done something that we can't get over or haven't done something that we should have. Maybe the absence of self-esteem or self-confidence since childhood is what keeps you stuck. Whatever the challenge is for you, in this section we are going to look at how you can begin to explore these issues to enable you to live a fuller, richer life.

The good news is that no matter what your life experiences have been, no matter what you have done, no matter what terrible experiences you have been through, things can change. If you really want things to change in your life, if you want to feel better, and if you are prepared to take personal responsibility for becoming the very best person you can be, then make a real effort with the material in this part of the book. By doing so, you'll begin to make headway in changing the shape and feel of your everyday life. I really believe everybody deserves this chance.

All you need for these exercises to begin to work for you is a willingness to change. You may not at this stage have any idea in the world of how you can do it; however, if you have the right mind-set you are almost 90 percent there.

In my workshops when I ask people to address change, I often experience strong resistance from them. What I have noticed is that people have real challenges with moving on. It's almost as if they have become too comfortable and attached to:

• people feeling sorry for them and the attention of being the victim;
• complaining about their lives and almost enjoying the pity;
• being judgmental and angry about their past and actually getting a kick out of feeling this way;
• keeping themselves down because it's easier than making changes;

• always saying they are frightened because it avoids failing or change; or
• holding on to guilt as it allows them to stay stuck.

On one level they really want to do something about making a change in their lives, but subconsciously it's as if they don't want to take the necessary steps to begin the process of change. It's almost as if the pattern that they have adopted through their negative life experience has become a friend, and letting it go or making a change involves a whole new way of living.

Is your way of dealing with life like a friend to you, or can you let it go?

Imagine if I were to say that tomorrow you could be free from the pain of your past. Imagine if I said that I thought you have suffered enough. Can you imagine giving this feeling up? If this were the case, how would you feel?

• Would your life feel empty?
• Would the space feel a bit frightening?
• What would you be free to do?

Now consider this: You actually have the power in this moment to flip that switch within you to make these changes happen for real. You have the opportunity to shed your old habit of suffering, worrying, and fearing the future. However, to make any kind of significant change, you must be willing to change and move on from this pain.

Sometimes when life is really tough, it's almost easier to stay in the place that is painful and familiar than to consider the hard work of making changes to improve our lives. I feel that when we become aware of this fact, we can become open to the possibilities of change.

On a scale of one to ten, how much do you want to change? If it is less than five, I would suggest that you pick up an escapist romantic novel and put this book down now—five won't work.

Case Study

Eleanor came along to my teacher-training college. I spotted her the second she came through the door. She wore a big black padded coat, and as the others relaxed into the warm, welcoming training room with its log fires and candles, Eleanor kept her coat on and her arms crossed. As the days passed, we began some intense work. Eleanor continued to wear the coat. As I worked through some exercises with her, I realized that she was holding on to so much from her past. She had barriers up in her life for everything, especially personal relationships. When I began to gently challenge her on the things that she was holding on to, I realized that she had formed many patterns in her life, and for her to change her life and her relationships for the better, this would have meant doing some really hard work. Her automatic response was to stay where she was—protected from the outside world, comfortable and safe.

By the end of day five, Eleanor had begun to realize that to move into a life that she loved and where she could experience happiness, she would have to consider letting go of the resentment and anger from her past. As she began the process, the coat came off—it was almost symbolic of the pain that she was holding on to—and the new Eleanor emerged. She had the support of ten others at the college, a counselor who was at the course, and myself.

"...shed your old habit of suffering, worrying, and fearing the future."

Be patient and gentle with yourself as you work through this material. If you recognize a real block that you are finding difficult to handle and that you feel this book doesn't address, phone a few professionals until you feel comfortable with someone who you think can help you. It may cost a little money, but consider how much you deserve to have some joy in your life. Joy is priceless, so be kind to yourself. You *deserve* it.

"One day as I heard my self complaining to my mom, I thought, *Dawn, if you want anything done, do it yourself.*"

BLAME

Blame is a perfect little device to avoid taking personal responsibility. When we can blame others, there is absolutely no need to question how we could have done something differently or better. When we blame everyone else, we don't grow in spirit or strength.

As well as taking personal responsibility for moving on from our past pains and hurts, it is often important that we get into the driver's seat of our lives. How often do you blame other people for your life not working out the way you really want it to? How often do you blame:

• your past experiences;
• your parents;
• your partner;
• your teachers;
• your religious upbringing;
• your schooling;
• yourself;
• your neighbors;
• the government; or
• God

. . . for the things in your life that don't work out? When we blame other people, it's often an automatic response to deflect any responsibility from ourselves. So often people get caught up in the habit of blaming everyone around them for everything that is going wrong in their lives.

EXERCISE

Think back over the last 24 months of your life. List all the disappointments that you have experienced in the different aspects of your life.

Relationships

Separation, divorce, breakdown in communication, falling out with friends, more . . .

1.

2.

3.

Health and Well-being

Illness, stress, depression, weight problems, giving up exercise classes, more . . .

1.

2.

3.

Time Out for You

Massage, relaxation time, hobbies, interests, vacations, more . . .

1.

2.

3.

Work Life

No pay raise, no promotion, getting laid off, business problems, more . . .

1.

2.

3.

When we constantly blame others, I believe we really feel out of control. I have a little motto in my life—if I want something done really badly, I just do it myself. I expect nothing from anybody; that way I am always in control of my own life and my own destiny.

Earlier this year I expected my local city council to fulfill a promise they made to me about disposing of some concrete from the back of my garden. Months went by and my neighbors began to get a little grouchy. The concrete was lying by the beach wall and after six weeks and repeated conversations with the local council, they still hadn't picked up the concrete. Eventually I felt the silent pressure from the neighbors escalate. I decided to take this into my own hands and hired a company to pick the concrete up, and then it was gone!

I spent weeks talking to everyone around me about the fact that the council had let me down, and I began to feel embarrassed that my neighbors were cleaning up the beach and that my trash was lying around. The whole situation began to take its toll on me. One day as I heard myself complaining to my mom, I thought, *Dawn, if you want anything done, do it yourself.*

So I did just that. When I took responsibility—
• there was no conflict with my neighbors;
• I wasn't on the phone complaining for hours; and

• I didn't have the continuing bad feeling about the local council.

Some people would disagree with me here and say that I pay my taxes, so I'm entitled to local government services. My argument is that if the anxiety is so great, I'm better off dealing with whatever needs to be done on my own. How much of your time do you spend blaming other people? How often do you blame your culture, the weather, the financial climate, your company, your boss, or your partner for the way your life is shaping up?

Do you always blame someone or something for your own failings instead of taking personal responsibility? I'd like you to be honest with yourself. Instead of blaming everyone and everything for what goes on in your life, ask yourself in what way were you personally responsible for each of these outcomes? What do each of these situations in your life say about you? What do you need to learn?

BE AWARE

There are some situations in life that we cannot avoid, like the death of a parent, a child, or a friend. In this situation you cannot be held personally responsible. Be careful not to be too hard on yourself for things that are out of your control.

Example 1

In my workshops, I regularly hear people say things like they don't exercise because their lives are too hectic and everyone else's needs always come before theirs. They don't have time to go to the gym, and everyone else is to blame.

Taking personal responsibility means that you recognize the need to put yourself first more often, and as a result of this, you make a commitment to setting aside time to exercise.

Example 2

Your relationship is breaking down because your partner never talks; they work long hours and you have no life.

In this situation you are blaming your partner. Taking personal responsibility would be to communicate your feelings to your partner and arrange the time to talk. Make it happen if you can; if not, take personal responsibility to create a new life for yourself.

Example 3

You haven't been promoted even though you work really hard, but a new high flyer in the department has come in and very quickly gained a promotion. You are angry at the situation and feel that your position has been undermined. In this situation you must question if you were really the best person for the job. What could you have done to ensure that the promotion was yours? Do you need extra qualifications or an improved attitude?

What do you need to learn from your experiences to ensure that in the future these outcomes won't happen again? Record what you find in your journal.

The world does not owe you a living. Life is what you make it, and life gives you what you put into it. If you take responsibility, and if you stop habitually blaming others and decide to embrace change, the future will be what you make it.

CHAPTER THIRTEEN

Learning to Love Ourselves Again

Self-belief is the internal power that can set you free. When you feel great about yourself, fear disappears and you can feel free to open your heart up wide and allow joy to come in and play in your life.

Do you:

- tell yourself off inside;
- think that you don't deserve love;
- live amid clutter and chaos;
- feed your body addictive substances and lots of things that aren't good for it;
- attract people who abuse you; or
- allow yourself to be walked over?

If you answer yes to any of these questions, then to make a real improvement in your feelings of well-being, it's important that you work toward getting your self-esteem and self-confidence firmly intact. I remember that the first time someone told me that I was suffering from low self-esteem, I didn't have a clue what it was. I had to look it up in the dictionary! It's funny—when you have buckets of it, there's no need to know what it is; but when you really don't have it, you need to find out how to create it. For some of us it can often just be a refocusing job, and for others it is a whole reprogramming effort, which will take a bit of time. So let me try to explain the difference between self-esteem and self-confidence, and then let's work through some exercises to help you develop it.

SELF-ESTEEM

People with high self-esteem generally feel good about themselves; they like who they are; they feel worthy of true happiness, real love, and good health; and they also believe they deserve forgiveness in their lives when they do something wrong.

When we have high self-esteem, we can experience the full enjoyment of life's beauty. When our self-esteem is intact, this sparks the self-confidence that we need to meet the challenges of life's journey. Self-esteem is a potent psychological and physiological quality that can heal and re-balance an exhausted mind, a tired body, and a clouded or suppressed sense of spirit.

SELF-CONFIDENCE

Self-confidence, on the other hand, is the energy that is created by your self-esteem. Self-confidence is like an anchor that allows you to stay strong when you need to communicate and interact with others, freeing you to move forward easily. When you have high self-confidence, you feel a strong sense of self-belief in all that you do. You are aware of what you are good at and what you aren't so good at, and you feel happy and content with that. Sometimes people say to me that as children they had no confidence or self-esteem and they believe that as adults this cannot change. I don't believe this for a moment. I have seen shrinking violets work at this stuff and become fully blossomed red roses, gentle to the eye but with the strength and determination inside to live life to the fullest.

Once again, it's not a magic potion that allows us to feel this way, it's just a matter of changing the habits that don't work for us in our lives and creating some new ones that do. The first step is actually becoming aware of what we think about ourselves, realizing how this can impact our relationships with others, and working from there.

LEARNING TO LOVE OURSELVES AGAIN

To love ourselves is to stand in front of a mirror and say *I like who you are as a human being.* To love ourselves is to say that our conscience is clear, our spirit is free, and on a deep level we are being true to ourselves and others.

When we really love who we are, we act and feel a bit like a young child. Do you remember as a child waking up in the morning with a clear conscience? You didn't even give your looks a second thought, you liked who you were and couldn't understand it if someone didn't like you! You were excited about your day, and there was absolutely no weight on your mind. You may have had a real feeling of internal freedom that, like a surge of electricity, bounced you out of bed each day to take on the world! As an adult, life experience kicks in, our self-beliefs and self-perceptions accumulate, and for most of us, the bouncing out of bed invariably stops. In this section I am going to give you some very simple coping strategies to begin your clearing process.

We need to look at what we believe about ourselves, and we need to question why we are shy, and why we walk with our backs slumped or our heads hanging down. (Who would ever think that a thought is what keeps your backbone straight!) We need to learn how to look in the mirror and like what we see . . . if we don't, how on earth can we expect anyone else to like us? Think about when someone loves us and begins to validate how we look. They tell us all the fantastic things that they see . . . our confidence is boosted, we begin to feel better, and life seems so much easier. We need to like ourselves to feel secure or we fall hostage to other people's responses. That leaves us vulnerable and insecure.

Can you relate to any of these?

• Do you focus on your bad points all the time?
• Do you put yourself down before others do it for you?
• Do you have feelings of lack?
• Do you worry about how you look all the time?
• Do you worry about what other people think of you?
• Do you keep quiet rather than speak up and feel vulnerable?
• Do you think you are boring or uninteresting?
• Do you dislike things that you do?

When we suffer from low self-esteem, the thoughts in our mind about ourselves are unsupportive, destructive, negative, and limiting. In our lifetime we can accumulate self-beliefs from other people's comments, views, statements, and beliefs about us. When we live with people or work in environments where people are negative, judgmental, and rude about us, the chances are that over a period of time we will begin to absorb and believe what we are hearing—sometimes without being aware of it. When we begin to play negative and destructive thoughts over and over in our mind, we ingrain them into our mind and lower our self-esteem.

Some people don't actually have to hear the negatives from others; they manage to constantly remind themselves of all that is wrong with them. I still believe, however, that it is possible to override the negative program with a positive one. It may just take a little more work.

EXERCISE 1

1. Think back to when you were a small child or when you were growing up.

Were you told by someone that you weren't deserving, and over a period of time you began to believe them?
Do you have a belief that to look after your own needs would be selfish?
Do you have a parent who was very unselfish and as a result your behavior has developed in the same way?
Do you have children? Often when we have children their needs become more important than ours. Have your needs become unimportant?
Did anyone ever tell you that you weren't good enough, or pretty or handsome enough?
Did anyone ever put you down? If so, why, and was it justified?

2. Record whatever you find in your journal.

Remember that people were only doing the best they could with the knowledge they had at the time when they treated you this way—please avoid blame.

Sometimes without even being aware of it, we can lose sight of the magic of who we are. Each one of us is unique, individual, and special, but sometimes the knocks and bumps can send us off track. Before we know it, we have almost forgotten who we are. When this happens, it can be a frightening feeling, but with a little mental readjustment to our beliefs and some changes to our habits, believe me, we can begin to get back on track again. In fact, if we work really hard at it, we can actually overtake where we once were and become the unique individuals we were born to be.

Sometimes when we have to cope with difficulties and challenges in life, we find that very quickly we can lose our self-esteem and self-confidence. If this confidence isn't repaired quickly, the feelings of lack, low self-worth, and fear can spread like wildfire into each and every area of our lives until we begin to feel fear in everything that we do.

THE FINGER!

I find it peculiar how the brain tends to focus more on our negative points than on what's positive in our lives. If we have one little thread of self-doubt, the brain focuses on it over and over

"The brain tends to focus more on our negative points than on what's positive in our lives."

again. Can you relate to this? I know this certainly happens with me. When I focus on my one little doubt, I feel a sense of vulnerability and somehow automatically begin to look for the next doubt until I get into a perpetual habit of focusing on all that is bad about myself.

I remember Spice Girl Geri Halliwell saying that one evening the group went to a George Michael concert. The girls were sitting at the side of the theater. George Michael announced that the Spice Girls were there that night, a huge searchlight beam went over to the little private boxes, and the crowd roared and cheered. As Geri looked out into the audience, she didn't see the hundreds of people clapping—instead she noticed one person sticking his middle finger up.

She says that out of all the millions of compliments she receives, she always remembers the one criticism. I can really relate to that comment, as I am sure you will, too. It seems much easier to remember the negative things than to remember what's good about us. I've been practicing affirmations for years now and it can still be tough.

The way to change these destructive thought patterns is to begin a process of overriding the self-doubt tapes that are playing in your brain by creating a powerful set of supportive affirmations.

You need to refocus your mind and do some exercises to remind you of your good points, throw some light onto your qualities, remind you of compliments that you may have received in your life, and of the good things that you have done. Step by step, you are gently going to begin to boost your self-esteem and self-confidence.

Let's get started . . .

LOOKING IN THE MIRROR

I mentioned earlier on in the book that during a training program I was asked to look into a mirror and tell myself that I loved myself over and over until I believed it. I found this so difficult to start with. I couldn't concentrate, and kept laughing! I really wanted this stuff to work, however, so I made a commitment to myself. With a little bit of practice, the technique began to sink in—yet another layer peeled off my onion!

I now realize that what I see in the mirror is an outer reflection of what I'm feeling about myself on a deep inner level. I wake up some days and feel perfectly content with my life, but I don't like the look of the face looking back at me—what some people might call a "bad hair day."

I'm aware that it's not always my thoughts that determine my bad hair days. I often feel that hormonal influences are kicking in, and sometimes, no matter how many affirmations I do, I really struggle to change the way I feel. I know that if things are a little rocky in my life, the face in the mirror isn't one I want to see.

Whatever I'm thinking and feeling about my life definitely has a huge impact on the way I see myself. When I'm feeling confident, sexy, and in control, I think I look amazing; and when I feel insecure and vulnerable, I feel that I look completely different.

". . . by looking into someone's eyes, you can see and read so much."

Have you ever stood in front of the mirror with tears rolling down your face, and as you did, your face almost felt like someone else's? You felt so disconnected from who you are. This feeling can last for a long time, and the only way to get reconnected is to look at the face in the mirror and feed yourself loving words until one day you begin to feel different. It may sound crazy, but it works. I believe that when we begin to treat ourselves gently and use nurturing words toward ourselves, almost as if we were positively encouraging a child, then we can begin to make progress and really feel a difference.

WE NEED TO CONNECT WITH OURSELVES AGAIN

There is something powerful, honest, and true going on when we feel we can look someone in the eye and make a commitment. When people fall in love, so much of their communication is done through looking into each other's eyes. The eyes really are the key to the soul, and by looking into someone's eyes you can see and read so much. If we can't look into someone's eyes, it's as if we are avoiding or hiding something. When people fall out of love, how often do they gaze at one another?

The same principles apply when we are looking at ourselves in the mirror. If we feel ashamed, unwilling, apathetic, self-critical, judgmental, dishonest about our own truth, or disconnected from our authentic joy, it will be very difficult to look into the mirror and say "I love you" or "I really like who you are."

To reconnect with our authentic self, we need to look at ourselves in the mirror and truly embrace the feeling of making a commitment to love and care for ourselves beginning today and from this moment forward. If you do this, you can begin to make great progress.

Start practicing by saying these affirmations 20 times or more each morning and evening.

- *Use a wall mirror or a hand mirror, making sure you can see your whole face.*
- *As you repeat the words, keep your focus on your eyes.*
- *Really feel the words as you repeat them.*
- *Sell the concept to yourself.*
- *Practice alone or you might face the prospect of being locked up!*

Here are some examples of affirmations that you might want to use:

I love you . . . , [your name].
I love you . . . , from today I am hailing you.
I love you . . . , from today I commit to taking care of you.
I love you . . . , I commit to making this life a joyful one for you, and you deserve the best.

Case Study

I remember in my training program 30 apprehensive multicultural faces looking at each other nervously as they were handed some little reflective hand devices to look into and tell themselves "I love you." Some giggled, others coughed, some turned away from the mirrors, some put the mirrors down and refused to participate.

Day one was tough and people were very uncomfortable, primarily because they had to tell themselves "I love you" for the first time in their life, and second they had to do it in a room full of 30 other people!

This was a lot to expect. As the week went on, we were expected to practice at home until we felt comfortable with the idea. Finally, by day five and having done about 2,000 "love you" affirmations, we were all feeling pretty comfortable and relaxed with ourselves. I think

we also felt excited at the prospect of living with this newfound feeling of self-esteem that we were beginning to nurture.

This stuff takes practice—don't give up! You may have spent years not liking or loving yourself, so as you begin this process it may feel uncomfortable, but please give it time and effort and you will reap the rewards.

WRITTEN WORK

Once you have chosen an "I love you" affirmation that suits you, the next step is to support it with a number of accelerators that will ensure that you really believe it.

Write down five accelerators to support your affirmation and pop it in your journal or on a sheet of paper and read it over and over until you feel really connected and comfortable with what you are reading. Read them at every opportunity. Here is an example:

I LOVE YOU . . . . [your name]

• *I am going to look after your needs from now on; you deserve to be loved.*
• *From now on I am going to do one special thing each day, just for you.*
• *You deserve some love in your life; it will feel warm again.*
• *. . . . . . . [name] says that you're wonderful. S/he means it! S/he can see it.*

Take out the photo of youself as a child. Look into the eyes of the little you and check from the list below how this little being deserves to feel—this little person who lives in you.

BE AWARE

Beware of thinking the pathetic thought that "there is nothing good about me, I can't fill this in." If you continue with this type of thought pattern you will always stay trapped. Please try to work really hard here . . . even if you can only come up with one or two of these statements, at least it's a start. Remember to look at your photo as you do this.

- I like me.
- I am a valuable human being.
- I am a beautiful human being.
- I have value.
- I am loving.
- I have so much to give.
- I have potential.
- I have worth.
- I am worth loving.
- I deserve to have fun in life.
- I am important.
- I am optimistic.

- I am lovable.
- I am unique.
- I am perfect exactly as I am.
- I deserve love.
- I deserve happiness.
- I deserve to be heard.
- I am caring.
- I am attentive.
- I am natural.
- I am kind.
- I am positive.

EXERCISE

Look at your photo as you complete the next exercise, then transfer your answers to your sheet or journal. This might be tough for you, so please be gentle with yourself. You might feel like giving up at this point, or skipping this exercise, or skimming through it. Don't! If you work really hard at these exercises, you will begin to feel some positive benefits. This is where you can now begin to create some positive dialogue that will anchor you and make you feel strong again.

I deserve to be happy because:

1.

2.

3.

I like me because:

1.

2.

3.

I am a valuable human being because:

1.

2.

3.

I am a beautiful human being because:

1.

2.

3.

I have value because:

1.

2.

3.

I have worth because:

1.

2.

3.

I am worth loving because:

1.

2.

3.

I deserve to have fun in life because:

1.

2.

3.

I am important because:

1.

2.

3.

I am lovable because:

1.

2.

3.

I am unique because:

1.

2.

3.

I am perfect exactly as I am because:

1.

2.

3.

Once you have completed the last exercise as best you can, record your statements into your journal and remind yourself daily of why you are so special. Come back in a few months to this exercise and complete it again.

COMPLIMENTS

Compliments are like little gift-wrapped parcels of love that people offer us when they believe within their hearts that we are worthy of them.

How often do you throw back compliments you are given by an admirer, boss, or a friend? This is such a common bad habit when our minds just cannot accept that someone wants to share something good about us. Become aware of how you react to compliments. Maybe from today you could practice saying "Thank you so much" when someone pays you a compliment; after all, don't you think it's a bit of an insult to someone's judgment if they give you a compliment and you automatically throw it back at them, insinuating that they are lying or being silly?!

TRY THIS!

List any compliments that you have had about the following:

Your face   Your mind   Your intelligence   Your creativity
Your eyes   Your abilities   Your personality   Your loyalty
Your smile   Your commitment   Your courage   Your potential
Your body   Your being a good mother   Your being a good father   Your being a good daughter
Your friendship   Your being a good son
Your sensitivity to others or animals

BE AWARE

Be aware of thinking the habitual self-critical thought that "there is nothing good about me; I can't fill this in." If you continue with this kind of thought pattern, you will always stay trapped. Work hard here, even if you can only come up with one or two. It's a start—go for it!

Once you have listed your compliments, write them down in a your journal and read them every day. Begin to build some really positive constructive dialogue in your mind. Remind yourself of your good points. Always record compliments in your journal as you receive them.

CHAPTER FOURTEEN

Clearing the Pain of the Past

- Forgiveness
- Releasing Guilt
- Living for Today
- Gratitude

When we clear out the pain and judgment that lurks inside us from our past, we feel freer and lighter. A weight is lifted from our hearts and souls, and there is a great new space for love and joy in our lives again.

Ask yourself the following questions.

Do you like yourself?
Do you have deep feelings of guilt about things that you have done in your personal/work life?
Do you carry guilt about a thing/things you haven't done?
Do you deeply resent someone?
Do you feel embittered about life?
Do you feel angry at God?
Do you criticize yourself and others?

If your answer to any of the above is yes, it's time to do a little bit of emotional clearing.

All of the above feelings and emotions are very common, and unfortunately they are the cause of many illnesses and diseases in our world. So often we believe that being angry, resentful, bitter, critical, or judgmental toward someone will have a negative impact on the other person; however, the reality is that if you continually react in this way the lasting negative effect will only be on you. As you constantly reinforce and refuel beliefs, habits, and emotions with large doses of anger or guilt, without being aware if it, these emotions will be having a daily impact on your body as well as your mind.

Let me give you an example.

RESENTMENT

If a woman is angry at her ex-husband for running away with his secretary, then chances are that for a long time she may play the scenario over and over in her mind. Will the ex and the secretary care, or will they be hurt by these feelings and emotions? The only person who is being hurt here is the woman who is feeling angry. Wouldn't it be so much healthier for her to let go of the pain?

GUILT

A woman loses her child. Understandably she finds it very difficult to move on in her life. Each day she lives with the guilt, not wanting to build a life for herself because her child is dead. It may sound harsh, but the dead child would want his or her mother to move on. The guilt is hurting the mother every day. Either she can hold on to the pain of the guilt and continue to believe that it is wrong to move on, or she can let it go and start really living again.

Case Study

DEALING WITH THE PAST

I worked with a beautiful young lady in a one-on-one session. She had attended one of my workshops and had done her affirmations and goals. She was excited about the prospect of change. At the workshop, she had worked through all her surface goals and aspirations; she even worked hard on building her self-confidence and self-esteem; however, during the workshop as she addressed vulnerability and truth, she continued to push down something that she didn't want to deal with. Two weeks after the high of the workshop, she began to feel down.

Although I don't usually do one-on-one sessions, I heard that she had called in tears and wanted to see me desperately. I made the time, and she came to spend the day with me. As I gently questioned her, the truth began to emerge. She had been raped and hadn't told a single soul in the world about it. I think that in her own mind this was the first time she had actually acknowledged what had happened to her.

I realized that for her to move forward with all aspects of her life, she really had to deal with this core issue. She desperately wanted to have someone special to love, but with this big dark cloud hanging over her, she could never move on.

After our session, I suggested that she contact someone for professional help. I know to this day that she still hasn't had the courage to make the phone call, and she continues to live in so much pain. She is so close to getting out of the trap, but the fear and the pain of her situation will keep her paralyzed, frightened, and single until she asks for help. Sometimes the most difficult thing is to admit that you need help, and it's so important to remember that whatever it might be, you don't have to deal with it alone.

What do you know that you need to deal with to move forward in your life? What black clouds are blocking your future happiness?

All of the above feelings create a negative, destructive charge in our souls. On a deep subconscious level, these feelings block our flow of joy and happiness, they stop us moving forward into the lives we want to live, and they keep us stuck in a place where we really don't want to be. These emotions can be destructive and painful and can keep us from moving forward. They hang around in our subconscious mind, so deeply ingrained that we don't even think about them or realize how much they influence our everyday actions and reactions to others.

In this section, we will explore dealing with deep feelings such as forgiveness, guilt, and resentment. We're going to look at how we can turn these emotions around so that we can begin to feel free from our past, allowing us to move into our futures with ease, feeling lighter and happier.

FORGIVENESS

Forgiveness heals sorrows and wounds, strengthens our souls, and offers us freedom. It's not something that makes us weak or vulnerable. When we learn to forgive ourselves and others, it is the biggest act of self-love and the greatest gift that we could ever give to ourselves.

When we forgive, we make a commitment to let go of the past. We can then begin to dissolve the present hurt and pain that we experience each day. When we begin the journey of forgiveness, we open the doors to love in our hearts again.

Willingness to forgive and to be forgiven can break down the prison walls that trap us in our lives. For some people, forgiveness occurs over a period of time, for others time doesn't heal the wound and new patterns and habits embed themselves firmly in place to ensure that there's no going back.

I believe that when we are harboring anger toward people, or when we are feeling deep feelings of guilt and pain from a past experience, these emotions can begin to resonate within our being. The energy of the emotion can build and accumulate inside you, creating illness. I have no doubt that these emotions clog the soul and by doing so have an impact on both our physical health and our future happiness.

I know that letting go is the toughest call in the world. When someone has hurt us, betrayed us, when someone has ripped our heart from our body by the way they have treated us, when we have been deceived, or when we feel the guilt of being alive when we lose a child, how on earth can we be expected to dust ourselves off and just get on with things? Surely it's human nature to hold on to this pain and never let go?

If this is how you feel, I am with you completely and I too realize that letting go is so much easier said than done, but there is one simple reason why you should consider letting go. If you don't, you will suffer until the day you die, and I don't think that is fair. Take out the photo of yourself as a little child and look right into the eyes of that innocent little person. Ask yourself the following questions:

• Does this little being deserve the pain that they are experiencing on a deep level each day, by not letting go of these emotions?

> "The energy of emotion can build and accumulate inside you, creating illness."

• Does this little child deserve forgiveness for what he or she has done? After all, we all make mistakes, don't we?

• Does this little being want to feel the deep emotion of love in his or her life? Imagine what it would be like to live a loveless life.

• Does this little being deserve to live a happy life? How could anyone put a stop to that?

Record in your journal what feelings come up for you in this exercise.

Suffering can become a habit that is difficult to give up. It can become our way of living and being, until we begin to make some fundamental changes in the way we live our lives and the way we think about ourselves and others.

NEUTRALIZING OUR EMOTIONS

If you really would like to change the way you feel inside, you can take a quantum leap in dealing with letting go of pain in your life by realizing that . . .

> people are only doing the very best that they can with the thoughts, habits, and behaviors that they have learned throughout their lives to survive in this world.

Someone told me once that you should try to feel compassionate toward the people you find most difficult to forgive or the people that you hate the most. At the time, I just

didn't get it! When I thought it through, I realized that forgiving someone and having generous thoughts toward this person was much better for me physiologically than having hateful thoughts about them. Then I got it!

When someone crosses you, betrays you, or really hurts you, it is so difficult to be kind to that person, let alone send them kind thoughts. Over a period of time, what we need to do in our own minds is work out why they might have done such a thing. Maybe . . .

• they were brought up with strong survival instincts;

• they saw their parents doing things like this;

• they did it because the boss wanted them to;

• they did it because they have a weakness in their character;

• they did it because they were frightened; or

• they did it because they were coerced.

When we take the focus off our own pain and reflect on what might lie behind someone's behavior, we can often begin to feel a bit more compassionate about the situation. If you can do this to the point where you accept the way that they are and you accept that what is done is done, in that moment you begin to free yourself from the pain and begin the process of letting go.

It's a tough one to deal with when we hear about pedophiles abusing children, kids being murdered, and marriages being wrecked by violence and cruelty. How on earth can we expect to understand what these people were doing? We want to kill them, and the feelings of anger burn like an inferno inside our hearts. But who's hurting from the emotion that you are feeling? Are they, or is it just you again?

To get our heads around this "pain-full" challenge we need to recognize that we will probably never understand such extreme behavior. We have to acknowledge that these people have been shaped by particular life circumstances and conditions, and need help badly. If we can change our mind-set from the emotion of anger to the emotion of sending love to someone who needs so much help, we can begin to neutralize our own emotions and feel much better internally. This is a self-protection mechanism that can be such a valuable tool.

The people I meet generally treat me with respect, and on the whole I would say that most people in my life are wonderful human beings. However, there is always the exception to the rule, and sometimes I have to deal with people whose behavior can be selfish, jealous, or critical. I have a little mechanism of accepting them exactly as they are, and I try with all my might to understand why they behave the way they do and why they treat other people the way they do.

Let me give you an example.

Who makes your blood boil? Have you ever met anyone who presses all your buttons? One particular person whom I know really "boils my blood." Each time I see him he presses all the right buttons to get me upset, and other people tell me they feel the same thing. This man is negative, cynical, and condescending. When I'm in his company, he makes sweeping generalizations that are detrimental to women, he makes rude comments about the people we are with, and generally he is unbearable. He cannot understand why he is alone and why people don't want to be with him.

He would love to find love and meet someone new, however his attitude is so appalling that this is unlikely. He constantly questions why other people have more luck than he does and why his glass is absolutely half empty and not half full. He actually speaks as if there were nothing in his glass at all! He is handsome, and he has a lovely home and some adorable children, but he continually focuses on what he doesn't have in life. He is envious of other peo-

ple, and although he is very proud of his kids, without even being aware of it he is critical and judgmental toward them, too.

As we journey through life, we will meet lots of people like this. We might even inherit them in our families, which is tough; however, it's a fact of life that we are going to need to learn to deal with them, so how on earth do we do it? I try to focus on how he has been shaped by his life experiences.

I can remember one day when I asked him if he was married, and he told me with venom how his wife left for another man about 15 years ago and how he had endured the struggle of bringing up two children on his own. He felt like he had been cheated out of a big chunk of his life. He implied that life had been so much easier before his wife left him, and through his anger I could see that he still had feelings for her. Although the odd family member was around, he's had a pretty tough run of it. The kids have now grown up and left home, leaving him embittered, sad, and lonely. Each time I am in his company I remind myself not to take his behavior personally—this is how he behaves with everyone he encounters. I feel sorry for him and send him love. This neutralizes my emotion. You have the potential to flip that inner switch! Try it . . .

What affirmation could you use to neutralize feelings of anger the next time you are with someone who makes your blood boil?

• *You are doing the best you can right now with the survival mechanism that you have developed to cope with life.*
• *I send you love—I can see you could use some help right now.*
• *I'm sending you love—you can't help the way you have become.*
• *You are doing your best—I send you love.*
• *You are doing the best you can with the knowledge/resources that you have at this time. I send you love.*

EXERCISE 1

What things do you feel you need to let go of in your life?
What experiences have made you fearful?
What has made you bitter?
What has made you angry?
What has ruined your confidence?

Consider the following:

Relationships	Friendships	Family	Siblings
Bosses	Colleagues	Parents	Children
Work	Health	Yourself	more . . .

Record what you find in your journal.

EXERCISE 2

What do you need to do to resolve or neutralize these emotions and feelings to ensure that your suffering/pain is reduced?

• What do you need to let go of?
• Whom do you need to forgive?
• Are you willing to begin this process?
• If so, list all the reasons why they may have done this thing. Practice neutralizing your emotion here if you can.

EXERCISE 3

Here are some general affirmations that have worked for others. Feel free to change and adapt and use them for yourself.

From this moment, I am willing to move forward in my life. I forgive with ease, in the knowledge that everyone is only doing the best they can with the knowledge that they have at the time. I am free.

From this moment, I am willing to move forward in my life. I release the past with ease. It's time for me to live my life right now. I now move into my new future where I have the keys to open any doors I choose.

I am now moving into my glorious new future. I have learned many valuable lessons from the past, and I now move on with hope and courage.

I deserve happiness. I am prepared to move on from this moment. I enjoy the magic of today; nature nurtures and nourishes me.

I swim in the magic of today, this is my miracle. I love life.

I deserve to live . . .

I choose life and life chooses me!

LETTING GO OF GUILT

When we decide to forgive others and ourselves, we make a decision to treat ourselves gently. When we treat ourselves gently, we can release ourselves from the pain of anger, shame, and guilt. We deserve this chance.

When we feel guilty, we are being tough on ourselves emotionally. Why is it that we don't treat ourselves gently, forgive ourselves, and move on? If we had a small child and they did something wrong, we wouldn't expect them to pay a lifetime's penance. So why is it as adults, when we do something that we consider to be wrong or when we feel bad about something, we can't let it go?

Perhaps it has something to do with our feelings about the difference between right and wrong. Although I believe that we should know the difference and should live in accordance with this, our existence on this planet is human, and that means that temptation and challenges will always be in our way. I feel that our humanity is what allows us to grow in strength and character. If we were all perfect, we'd have no learning or growing to do.

Perfection is not human! So when we make a mistake, as long as we learn from it and make sure we don't repeat it, we need to give ourselves a big break and let ourselves off the hook—for now at least. If you are someone who has repeatedly done things that you shouldn't have, you have a choice right now—in this moment you can make a change and begin to live a life that feels guilt free.

Feeling guilty is the biggest waste of energy in the world, and it serves absolutely no purpose at all. You can feel guilty all you like about things that have happened in your past—no amount of guilt will ever change a single thing in your life. It will only make you feel bad.

Do you feel guilty about:
• having done something that you believe is very wrong;
• being disrespectful to others;
• getting drunk;
   • taking drugs;
      • sleeping with someone you didn't love;
      • eating chocolate;
      • living when someone else is dead;
   • not having said how you felt to someone who is dead;
• having committed fraud;
• cheating on someone you love;
• sharing someone's deepest secret; or
• telling a lie when you should have told the truth?

If you live with feelings of guilt, you will know what it is like to feel stuck and trapped, constantly feeling bad about all that you have done, or all that has happened to you. You can choose in this moment to begin to free yourself: Right now you can start to deal with it, or you can carry it around every day, perpetuating the habit. The choice is yours.

We have a number of choices in dealing with the guilt in our lives.

• We can accept that the situation has happened and accept that there is nothing that we can do to resolve it

• We can learn a lesson from our experience and try to ensure that it never happens again?
• We can apologize or say we're sorry to help alleviate the feeling, knowing that you have done the best you can to resolve the situation.
• We can send some sort of acknowledgment to relieve our sense of guilt.

The Serenity Prayer

"Lord grant me the serenity to accept the things I cannot change; the courage to change the things I can; and the wisdom to know the difference."

This little prayer contains the most powerful three lines I know. If we can grasp the essence of it, we can begin to make some lasting changes in the way we feel, and it is particularly appropriate for dealing with guilt.

Let's take a look at what it really means.

SERENITY PRAYER LINE 1

"Lord grant me the serenity to accept the things that I cannot change."

There are so many things that happen to us in our lives that we cannot change, and as time passes, we find that as painful as certain experiences are, they are beyond our control. However much it might hurt, we really have to learn to accept them. Here are some examples of things that we might consider accepting, since once they are done, there is no way of undoing them.

• When a loved one dies and we haven't said what we wanted to say
• When someone is diagnosed with a terminal illness
• When someone has had an affair
• When a relationship ends and there is no going back
• When someone has a disability/disfigurement
• Getting older

Think of others that are appropriate for you.

Holding on and trying to fight against the tide of life can be exhausting and wearing. It can bring us to our knees, and in our desperation to find answers and avoid pain, we try to change things that we will never on this earth be able to change. In this section, we are going to look at how we can create some peace to quiet the inner turmoil that we often feel when we haven't accepted situations that occur in our everyday lives.

SERENITY PRAYER LINE 2

"Give me the courage to change the things I can."

In this statement, we consider what we really need to deal with to make life feel better.

So often the fear of dealing with difficult situations can feel daunting, and it takes a huge amount of courage to take the first step, but when we find that courage and begin to deal with whatever it is, the flow of life becomes much easier.

How often have you thought that you really should deal with something but you just keep putting it off? How often have you considered that you really must make a change, but lack of courage has stopped you from doing what you know you would like to do?

In this line, we see that we need courage if we want to feel better. Let's look at a few examples.

• Let go of the past
• Forgive someone
• Change your mind-set to accept the things you didn't believe you could
• Resolve conflict in difficult relationships
• Speak up for yourself
• Go for counseling to deal with painful emotions
• Say you're sorry
• Change something in your relationship(s)
• Change your state of health/well-being
• Change something about your work
• Change the way you live your life

What do you need courage for in your life? If you can find the courage to do the things you need to do, then you can begin to change the way you feel. Guilt, pain, anger, and bitterness all clog up your spirit and create a negative charge in your emotions and your physiology.

SERENITY PRAYER LINE 3
"Give me the wisdom to know the difference."

So often we believe that we can change things that we just can't. We cannot undo the past, and we cannot influence the fate of something that has already happened or is already happening in our lives. Conversely, sometimes we think that what is done is done and certain things cannot be changed when, with a bit of effort, there is still a chance that a certain situation may be resolved.

Here are some examples:

When a doctor diagnoses a terminal illness, you will probably be told that statistically you have a certain percent chance of survival. There are always variables in statistics, and with the right focus on your mind, body, and spirit, there is a possibility of being able to heal.

If you have an argument with a friend and you both stop contacting each other, you might think that the friendship is over. It may not be, however, as it is always possible that one of you can say you're sorry and start to heal the relationship. If someone's child is taking drugs, trying to keep the child away from their friends and what might already be an addiction is not the answer. The parent can't change the situation, and must accept that all he or she can do is support the child—they themselves must want to begin to face up to and deal with their drug habit.

When someone close to you has died and you realize that you didn't say what you should have said to them, there is no going back. No amount of guilt will ever change this situation. It's in the past and you must now endeavor to move on.

EXERCISE 1

1. What situations in your life do you feel you need to let go of or accept to quiet the storm of emotions in your mind or the pain in your body?

2. What would you like the courage to deal with in your life? (Really dig deep here.) In your journal make a list.

EXERCISE 2

This week why don't you write a letter or note to the person you feel guilty about. It may be:
• a love letter to someone you cheated on;
• an honest letter to a dear friend;
• a letter to yourself, from your guardian angel to advise you on how to change;
• a partner you have left;
• someone you have stolen from; or
• whatever feels right for you . . .

Tell them in the letter absolutely everything you are feeling. Tell them everything that is tucked away at the bottom of your heart and soul. Really be honest and say how sorry you are for what you have done. Get it all out as if you are doing an emotional and mental clearing-out. It may be tough to get started; however, once you get going, you may not be able to stop! Once you have completed this, you may wish to:
• bury it in a special place;
• wrap it in a ribbon and keep it in a safe place;
• keep it in your journal;
• burn it and let the emotions go;
• and if you are really courageous why not send it . . .

The purpose of this letter is to get all of our internal emotions out. It is a great opportunity to see what you are storing deep down in your subconscious. You will be able to see exactly what you are holding on to and how you may be criticizing and judging yourself. It may be revealing to you, and as you do it, you may realize what you need to let go of to move on and unclog your spirit and soul, not to mention to begin to heal and repair your body.

EXERCISE 3

So often we carry guilt around and then find ourselves repeating the behavior that makes us feel guilty. In order to let go of continuing feelings of guilt, we must ensure that we learn valuable lessons from the repeated behavior that makes us feel guilty. Then we must ensure that we learn from these lessons and break the habit of behaving in the same way again.

What habits do you have that repeatedly make you feel guilty?
1.
2.
3.

What do you need to remind yourself of to break these habits?
1.
2.
3.

List what you find in your journal, or make up some powerful affirmations in order to support yourself and retrain your thinking.

CHAPTER FIFTEEN

Living for Today

"Yesterday is History
Tomorrow a Mystery, and
Today is a Gift.
That's why it's called the Present."

This is another little quote that I believe has
tremendous value. We acknowledge that what is
done is done; we cannot change it, and the past is
over and done with. Tomorrow can be whatever we
choose it to be; a mystery that is yet to be revealed. We
have great influence over our tomorrows, and if we become
aware of how we are thinking and behaving, our tomorrows
can be fantastic and bright. The choice is ours.

Today is the "present," a beautiful gift that we should give thanks for and be grateful for every single day. We should acknowledge the fact that we are alive, we have food on our table and we are healthy and safe. I truly believe that when we look around us we have so many reasons to be happy; however, the habit of focusing on what we don't have prevails. What are you grateful for today?

So many people spend their days in emotional turmoil. They worry about what has happened in the past, they may worry about what could happen in the future, they feel guilty about things that have happened that they could easily influence, and they feel guilty about things that they could never do anything about. The final result is that the Gift of Today is lost in the pain and conflict of emotional turmoil that they feel they cannot resolve. It doesn't have to be this way.

There have been times in my life when I felt that everything was falling down around my ears. I have felt emotionally drained and stressed, I've had bills piling up all around me, and I've had unresolved issues clouding my mind all day long. At times like this it was really difficult to find anything positive in my day, however unbeknownst to me I was surrounded by joy, but I'd just lost sight of it. My daughter was healthy, I lived on the beach, I had great friends, I was managing my debt, I was healthy and well—yet I couldn't see any of these truths. I discovered a fantastic little tool called the Gratitude Journal, and it slowly began to refocus my whole outlook on life. All I had to do was take ten minutes each day. Each morning, I would light a candle and list 20 things that I was grateful for. Starting the exercise was difficult, but soon I began to write with ease.

EXERCISE 1

The Gratitude Journal

In your journal or in a separate little book, record a note every day of 20 things in your life that you are grateful for. List the simple things, from being able to pay your bills to the more complex ones like having patience in certain situations or doing something really well. Do this for 30 days. Choose from things like:

- Paying the bills today
- My child's health
- My good health
- Having money in the bank
- Having a home

- Having a job
- Having a beautiful friend
- Being able to trust someone
- Being able to support my child
- Having children

"We should give thanks and be grateful for every single day."

Try it for yourself. This is a beautiful way to change a negative, clogged-up mind-set into one of joy, happiness, acceptance, and love.

When we do this exercise, it begins to refocus our thoughts away from lack and toward gratitude. When our minds are full of what we don't have, there is no space to focus on what we do have. When things are tough and we feel that all hope is gone, this is a comforting little technique that allows us to gently refocus. At the end of your 30-day period, look back and actually absorb all the great things about your life.

I believe the most well-rounded people I have met are those who have been through difficult changes and situations and come through them stronger and more interesting. The tough stuff builds our character; it shapes us as human beings, and how we deal with it is what defines us. We can lie down and let it take over our lives, or we can take control back into our own hands. You can do this alone, in a group, or with a counselor—what matters is that you recognize something has to change and at that point you begin to do something about it. Be under no illusion—change is tough, but the rewards once the storm settles are rich. I promise—I've done it!

EXERCISE 2

List three of the biggest challenges that you have dealt with in your life (you can list more if you want to):
1.
2.
3.

Now write down how you have grown in strength and character from this experience. List what you find in your journal and remind yourself of it regularly. Refocusing on gratitude in this way helps strengthen your spirit.

Some examples may be:

- You can now help others
- You got to know yourself
- Your confidence improved
- You hadn't realized how resilient you were
- You realize how strong you are
- You know you're a survivor

- You learned valuable life lessons
- You became more self-sufficient
- You got stronger
- It made you more determined
- You now know that you can deal with anything
- It gave you the biggest nudge to embrace life

What did it do for you?

Lifelines to the New You

SAYING NO

When we are in control of our lives, we don't have to learn how to say no. I have to admit that not saying no to people used to be one of my greatest weaknesses. If someone asked me to do something, even if there was an internal inferno blazing inside me and I wanted to scream "No way," I would still do what was asked. By not speaking my mind, I have felt walked over, violated, used, and abused, and all of these feelings are very difficult to live with. I have felt ashamed of myself as people dominated and manipulated me. I was actually giving them a license to hurt me by not speaking up for myself. By saying yes once, you begin to set up a pattern, and people very quickly learn to take advantage of you. Unless you stick to your guns, people will continue to treat you like this, and as a result, nothing will change.

When you say no once or twice, people begin to get the message, and it's amazing how very quickly they begin to change their responses to you. Until you try it, you will never know how this works. It's like magic. Soon, everyone is treating you with respect. So let's look at how we can begin to change this and create a new habit.

SAYING NO TO PEOPLE IS AN ART

As human beings, we need to interact with others. To live life, we need to communicate; how we communicate and treat others often depends on how we have been treated by our parents and the people around us. Some people have loved us, supported us, stimulated and encouraged us, and have created positive influences in our lives. We feel that it's easy to communicate with these people. Other people somehow make us feel uncomfortable, upset, stressed, anxious, and afraid. Unfortunately, there is no way of avoiding these people in our daily lives. They may be:

- friends who tease or dump on us;
- parents who restrict or dominate us;
- an overbearing mother-in-law;
- a bullying or aggressive boss; or
- a partner whom we have perhaps fallen out of love with;

Who else can you think of?

Sometimes we wish that those who hurt us or caused us to feel stressed would just disappear. There are times when we wish that we could confidently stand up to them and tell them what we think . . . if we only had the courage. Sometimes we imagine a scenario in which we say all the things we would absolutely love to say, but we are always our own worst enemies as we continually do what they want us to do, or we don't say what we need to say to avoid confrontation. The fear of confrontation arises, and we worry that it will result in:

• being fired;
• being hurt mentally or physically;
• being dumped;
• being abandoned; or
• having a massive argument.

So instead we remain passive, and we never get what we want, we never get heard, and people continue to walk all over us. I used to think that to say what I needed to say I had to become more aggressive, but this isn't actually the case. To become more assertive means to become less passive. To become more assertive, we need to communicate more clearly and more directly; we need to become able to say no, and when we begin to behave in this way, within a few days people begin to notice a change and begin to treat us differently. You would be amazed at the difference. However, you must remain consistent, stick to your affirmation habits, and be careful not to fall into old behavior. It would be wrong for you to sacrifice your needs and the needs of your family by constantly saying yes when you really want to say no! It is actually possible to say no without saying no! The alternative is to offer a solution that gives you what you need without creating an overly aggressive response.

Example 1

Your boss always asks you to do things that aren't actually your job. You are tired of being the office patsy and being walked over. What can you do? You are frightened of losing your job or being ostracized by people at work.

AGGRESSIVE RESPONSE

"I'm not doing this anymore. I'm the general scapegoat in this place, and I'm fed up with it. You guys treat me like dirt."

ASSERTIVE RESPONSE

"I have so much on my plate right now. Would there be any possibility of Anne and Keith helping with the extra responsibilities? I'm sure you understand. I'm struggling to find enough hours in the day at the moment."

As soon as you become proactive, as soon as you begin to find solutions, you will begin to break down the old habits. If you continue to take everything on board, nothing will change.

Example 2

A demanding, elderly housebound mother asks her daughter if she's coming by on

Sunday for tea. The daughter has only one opportunity in the week to spend time with her husband and children, and looks forward to this special family time together at home. When the mother asks whether she is coming, the daughter wants to scream, "NO!"

AGGRESSIVE RESPONSE

"I can't ever have a weekend with my own family because of you. Why don't you spend time with one of my sisters this week? Why must it always be me?"

ASSERTIVE RESPONSE

"Mom, I really must have some time with the family; we haven't done it in ages. Sister or friend might want to stop by for a change. Why don't I call them for you? (In this situation, you are being helpful, reasonable, and constructive.)

Example 3

Say you want to complain or be heard about something you are unhappy with, such as:

• cold coffee in a restaurant;
• an overpriced bill from the garage.

In this situation you should:

• make your comment calmly;
• state the logic of the request without being emotional; and
• state your preferences.

If you feel you aren't being heard, say that you will take the matter to a supervisor, a manager, or even to a governing body. The more you practice this new habit, the easier it becomes.

SETTING GUIDELINES … AND NOT BREAKING THEM

Setting personal guidelines helps you attract the right people and the right situations into your life. When you feel that you deserve love and respect, and you set up personal guidelines, people can't treat you badly any longer. When you don't respect yourself or you believe you aren't deserving, you are not treated with respect, and you don't get what you want.

What we believe we deserve in life is exactly what we get. When we have high expectations and strong personal boundaries, we are safe. This is a tough lesson to learn. People often say to me that in every job they do they're bullied, every relationship they have they're abused; somehow they are always treated disrespectfully. Have you ever wondered why? Often we attract situations into our life because we don't have a set of guidelines from in place to prevent the negative situations arising.

When emotional parenting works well, children have strong values about how they should live their lives. As well as core values, the child has a set of guidelines on how to treat others and how to expect others to treat them. For some people, these lessons are like a muddy pool, and their life experiences have clouded the waters to the point where they have no guidelines in place.

I often ask people to see their guidelines as a fence that protects them from the outside world. It is a sad fact of life that people will violate your space if you have difficulty keeping them out, or if you have nothing in place to protect you. When this happens, we find ourselves in difficult situations that we can't get out of, we feel frustrated and sometimes frightened. When we do eventually get out of the situation, we feel relieved—and then usually it will happen again, sooner or later. Why? It's your thoughts and repetitive habits that are making your life shape up this way.

When we allow people to treat us badly, we may feel victimized, bullied, let down, or walked over, which can be distressing and even dangerous. Until we uproot these beliefs and clarify what they are, we will continue to attract difficult situations into our life. If this resonates with you, we have to work hard to establish a strong set of beliefs and behavior that will make sure you don't find yourself in this place again. Unless you set your guidelines, nothing will change. The first and second time your behavior changes, people will continue to try their luck, so you must stay true to yourself and stick to your guidelines. The third time they don't succeed in treating you in a certain way or they aren't getting what they want, they will give up and go somewhere else.

Here are some examples of beliefs and thoughts that can get you into a lot of hot water.

DATING

• I'm not really attracted to him, but if he thinks I'm cute, then he must be nice.
• I think he's rude, but he's paying attention to me, so I'll go with it.

"What we believe we deserve in life is exactly what we get."

• He doesn't really respect me, but he buys me a drink sometimes so I'll go out with him.

• If I sleep with him just this once, he might want to see me again.

BEING WALKED OVER AT WORK

• I'm scared to say no in case I'm tired, so I'll do it this once.

• If I don't do it, no one else will, so I'd better!

• What if he/she gets mad if I say no?

• If I speak my mind, I may offend him/her, so I'd better stay quiet.

ABUSIVE PARTNER

• He/she says he/she loves me; I am sure this person won't do it again.

• Next time I'm leaving.

• Aggressive behavior toward others protects me.

• Aggressive behavior toward others is manly.

• Aggressive behavior toward others is sexy.

If your personal or work relationships always repeat themselves, then you need to take a good look at what you are thinking or doing to attract these situations. Until you make a change, these painful feelings won't go away.

EXERCISE
Let's Begin to Write Your Guidelines for Life

Imagine you are writing these for your own child or for the little child in your photo. This might feel tough and unrealistic for you; however, until you begin to change what you think about yourself and how this is impacting your habits, you will be firmly stuck in your rut. If, however, you rewrite the script and begin to act in a new way, life can be so different.

1. In a journal, record what you find. List what you deserve and how you deserve to be treated:

• In a marriage
• On a date
• In a relationship
• At work
• By your boss

• By your friends
• By your peers
• By your parents
• By your partner
• By your children

2. Once you complete this, write an affirmation for each with the reasons why you deserve to be treated this way.

3. List what things you need to do to make changes in your life to ensure that you are respecting yourself and others are respecting you.

Good luck with this one; it's a toughie and will take a bit of time. Share your thoughts and findings with a really supportive friend and ask him or her to encourage you as you begin a new routine.

CHAPTER SIXTEEN

Connecting with the World

To connect with others is to feel alive. Connection with others is essential if we are to heal our wounded hearts and continue to grow. Connection is the firework that can set our souls on fire. Love is the greatest connection of all. When we love others, this allows our hearts to sing, and to be loved is the greatest prize of all.

Do you blush when you walk into a room full of strangers?

Do you feel paralyzed by the prospect of speaking in public?

Do you feel frightened to walk into a bar or a restaurant on your own?

Do you miss out on opportunities because you feel too shy to try new things?

Do you walk into public places and think that everyone is watching you?

I used to think that some people were shy and others weren't. The truth is that most of us feel pretty apprehensive on the inside in situations that are new to us—it's just how we deal with the shyness that differs from person to person. People who meet me would say that I'm incredibly confident, but I often quiver in my shoes when I have to meet new people. When I get up onstage to speak to audiences of 500 to 1,000 people who are eagerly waiting to hear what I have to say, I often feel nervous and sometimes sick to my stomach. When I run a workshop with 12 people, I can feel just as nervous because I don't know the people who are sitting down in front of me. To the outside world, no one would know how I'm feeling, as I have mastered my internal communication to such a degree that when I find myself shaking in my shoes I just give myself a

really good talking to. I affirm and affirm and affirm!

So many people feel that being too shy holds them back. So often we reveal our shyness in our physiological reactions. We may feel sick and turn pale, we may get sweaty palms, we may get a red rash on our neck, or we may blush so much that our face looks like a tomato! All of these reactions come from a thought or a series of thoughts that are running around in our heads. Your familiar gremlins are at work, telling you something that is going to scare the living daylights out of you in this situation. So our challenge here is to begin to reprogram the gremlins and begin to build some new habits into our lives that will help us combat and overcome the fear.

I can remember wearing a neck scarf for the first year of running my workshops, as my neck would give my nerves away each time I stood up in public. Inside I'd be falling to pieces and on the outside I was trying to compose myself as best I could. The scarf was part of my mask!

WHEN WE BLUSH

A red face comes from a thought that is activating the physiological system. The next time you blush, ask yourself:

What am I thinking in this situation? It may be that you are thinking:

• *You have found me out.*
• *You are looking at me in a funny way.*
• *I can't deal with this.*
• *Yikes! What am I going to do now?*
• *You are better than I am.*
• *You actually know more than I do.*
• *Am I boring you?*
• *I'm petrified in this situation.*
• *Maybe you know what I am thinking.*

The mechanism to stop this reaction is to identify the thought you are having and begin to override it with the opposite thought or an affirmation, and then repeat it over and over again until you override the existing program in your brain.

I remember being asked to speak to 500 employees, managers, and consultants at a Learning for Life seminar at Heriot-Watt University in Edinburgh. One of the speakers had dropped out at the last moment and I was asked if I could fill the slot. I was very busy at the time, and without really thinking it through, I accepted.

"I used to think that some people were shy and others weren't. The truth is that most of us feel pretty apprehensive on the inside in situations that are new to us."

I wasn't sure about the context of my talk in relation to the seminar, and as I drove toward the university, I naturally began to feel a bit apprehensive. At the entrance, I began to feel sick to my stomach. In my head, I was imagining that my talk would be out of context and no one would really have a need for what I was going to say. I was feeling tired, and when you are speaking to a large group of strange faces, to capture the audience's attention you must put on a bit of a performance. My nerves were kicking in. I had been traveling a lot, and because I was pretty exhausted, my resistance was low; then a sense of panic set in. I started to imagine making a fool of myself and all the worst-case scenarios that could arise on this big stage. Then the tears began. I sat in my car, desperately wanting to turn back and cancel my talk, but my pride was too big for that. However, here I was sitting in my car thinking, *I can't do this.*

I had no choice: I had to do it. I stopped crying and thought to myself, *You can do this,*

Dawn, you have done this kind of thing so many times before and it has always been a success. What is the worst thing that could happen? And if it happened, could you deal with it? Of course I could handle this. I fought the gremlins in my head. I started to repeat out loud: *You can do this and you are going to enjoy it. You can do it.* In the car I reapplied my makeup. I took a deep breath and walked toward the conference venue. As I walked, I held my head up high, I felt my back really straight and I smiled. THE POSITIVE VOICE WAS BOOMING IN MY HEAD. As I reached the conference-room door, I was met by the executive who had booked me and I confidently shook her hand. She asked how I was feeling and I said, "Excited!"

I had 15 minutes during which everyone was having a break to get a sense of the room. I walked up and down, I sensed the space, and in my head I was running images through my mind of me talking and making people laugh and smile. I had totally squashed the pictures that had been in my mind 30 minutes earlier.

VISUALIZING MY SUCCESS

As well as running the thoughts through my mind, in this situation I really did have to imagine myself up on that stage, I had to create a compelling vision of my success. I could almost touch the images that I was playing over and over, and if we think back to the head-turning exercise, this was releasing the feel-good endorphins into my system. It was important to see the image in my mind of connecting with people and making them laugh, to visualize my whole outcome. The words were encouraging me to feel good, but if in my mind I had an image of failing, this would probably override all my positive affirmations. It was therefore important to create a strong image of success to feed my subconscious all the right signals and ensure that my energy and emotions were absolutely on track for my performance.

Here's the affirmation with the accelerators that I used.

• *Dawn, you are a brilliant presenter, you can do this:*
• *Remember other big occasions when you conquered your fear and you were great—remember those feelings.*
• *You can flick this switch and SQUASH the gremlins. Do it.*
• *It's great to be invited to speak here—be enthusiastic, be genuine, and just be you.*
• *Trust that you are not alone—you are doing this work for all the right reasons.*
• *Someone out there really needs what you are about to say. You can help.*

As it turned out, this was the most successful seminar I had done so

"A smile *is the most* beautiful *form of silent communication."*

far. We booked a lot of business and so many opportunities opened up for me.

Many people are shy and nervous in all sorts of situations, but I believe the best opportunities go to the ones who manage to master their internal communication. This is a habit that can be nurtured if you are willing to work on it.

If you feel shy or nervous in certain situations and you find it difficult to communicate with people, what you need to do is create a new habit that will enable you to practice making simple contact with other people. Try these!

SMILE

When we walk around outside, we often keep our head down and don't connect with other people. This week, try to make eye contact and smile at people you don't know and haven't spoken to before. You can do this with anyone. Begin where you feel most comfortable, then move out of that comfort zone over the next four weeks.

Give it a try. What is the worst thing that can happen?

A smile is the most beautiful form of silent communication—you can light up someone's day without even saying a word. Really absorb

how it feels to accept a smile back. It feels so good. Count how many smiles you can collect in one day!

In your mind, practice an affirmation that feels comfortable for you, such as:

"You look like you would enjoy a smile, catch this."

"Hello, you look nice, I'd just like to show you."

"Isn't this a wonderful world. I feel free."

"I love connecting with the world and everyone in it."

Try this:

With men	With women
With old people	With children
With animals	On the bus
In the office	In the street
In the gym	In stores
In the streets	In the park
In a bar	

SAY HELLO

I live in Joppa on the outskirts of Edinburgh, a typical suburban city environment where people don't really know each other and often you don't even know your next-door neighbor. My house is by the sea, and there is a promenade that I'm sure was designed for daily exercise. There are people out rollerblading, cycling, jogging, and then there are the less energetic ones—the fast walkers, like me. When the weather is right, it feels like the most beautiful place in the world. When I first went out fast walking, I felt really self-conscious in my shorts, sneakers, and T-shirt. If I saw someone on the sidewalk, I would sometimes cross over to the other side of the street, keep my head right down, and avoid eye contact or saying good morning to a stranger at all costs. My little circuit of running around the housing estate, along the promenade and down the main street, felt like a very insular regime and a whole lot of hard work.

One day I woke up and decided that to make this hard work easier, I needed to change my routine. I was bored doing the circuit this way, and it was now time for a bit of an adventure. I decided that I would connect with every single person I met—man, woman, young, old, happy or sad—and say "Good morning" regardless of whether they smiled or not. Initially I was nervous and apprehensive. I could feel myself sizing people up and anticipating the outcome before I said anything, but I found that people always smiled back or said good morning in return. To be honest, I think they liked it—wouldn't you? I felt that a new world had opened up. Each day at the same time I'd head off. Everyone was in

their own little daily routine, in the same place at the same time. Each day I said good morning, and eventually the good mornings were returned with some other greeting or positive comment about my exercise routine as people became more familiar with me. It was a lovely feeling.

It's interesting to look back at how disconnected I was from people in my local area when I started this routine. Now, a year later, I say hello to the butcher, the postman, the old man with the big black cat, and the little old lady who has been doing her shopping at the same time at the same store for the last 40 years. When I go out for a walk with my daughter, I see lots of familiar faces and talk to so many people. It's great how you can open up your world with a smile and one hello! By giving and receiving a simple greeting, you can begin to feel less isolated and be more a part of something new. Why not try building a routine into your life and start saying hello . . .

At the gym
While running
On the bus

At church
When walking the dog
In stores
. . . and more

Once you have completed the smile exercise, challenge yourself and begin to say hello. If you feel up for it, begin this right away. Open up your world. This is just a new habit for you to practice!

EXERCISE—BOOSTING YOUR SELF-CONFIDENCE

Work through these exercises to improve your self-confidence in situations you may find difficult.

List some situations where you have felt shy to begin with, but they worked out okay for you in the end.

1.

2.

3.

In what situations do you feel really shy?

1.

2.

3.

What do you imagine is going to happen in each of these scenarios?

1.

2.

3.

Go back to the above, and circle any that are habitual, fearful thoughts or habitual gremlins in your mind—False Expectations Appearing Real

What thoughts would you have running in your head in these situations? (List as many as you can.)

1.

2.

3.

Now change these thoughts into positive affirmations, remembering to keep them in the present tense, using personal, positive words and powerful statements.

1.

2.

3.

Try this every morning and evening to begin to override the programs running through your mind. Do this constantly before going into what feels like a difficult situation. See the picture of the positive outcome in your mind; visualize and feel yourself experiencing a really successful outcome. Run the images over and over and support them with the affirmations until the picture is clear.

Here are some general affirmations that you might like to use to help you overcome shyness or to boost your confidence in difficult situations. You may wish to write some accelerators to support these statements. Think back to when you have conquered this feeling in the past, and record it.

I release the need to worry about
*   what other people think—I am free.*
I can now deal with any situation—
I feel relaxed.
I feel confident right now—I am calm.
I am always enough, just the way I am.
I am relaxed.
I feel comfortable being me. I am calm.
I'm now giving people the chance to get to
*   know me.*
Life is so much easier now that I feel relaxed.
I am calm and relaxed, I am just me, and that's
*   okay.*

I feel relaxed; I smile and say hello easily.
I think calm thoughts; I feel calm and relaxed.
People are interested in each other. I am not the
*   center of the universe when I walk into a room.*
Think back to the lemon exercise and imagine the physiological impact that these thoughts can have on you if you find yourself in difficult situations. This is how to reverse sweaty palms and red rashes! To try this out, instead of waiting for the next difficult situation to arise, do something out of your comfort zone this week, such as:

• Talk to a stranger
    • Volunteer to hold a meeting
        • Speak to someone you admire
            • Offer to take responsibility
                • Speak to someone new when you pick the kids up
                • Speak to a neighbor you don't know
            • Strike up a conversation with the butcher
• Stand at the front of the aerobics class
• Talk to someone at the gym
• Do a reading at church
• Collect for a charity

BREATHING NEW LIFE INTO YOU

When we feel like we're carrying the world on our shoulders, a big slice of what we love goes a really long way. When we do what we love, our heart jumps for joy. Our internal pharmacy shouts with delight, and our soul and spirit are free to fly.

When life takes its toll on us, it's really difficult to focus on what we love to do. Our mind-set is turned in the opposite direction, and it can be hard to think about what we love to do.

I believe that to heal and repair a bruised and tired soul, we need to nurture it and replenish its energy with a lot of whatever it is that really lights our fire. Sometimes we can forget what makes us happy because we haven't done it for so long.

> "I believe that to heal and repair a bruised and tired soul, we need to nurture it and replenish its energy with a lot of whatever it is that really lights our fire."

When we look at creating some real quality time, we need to take quite a selfish view. This time is for you and you only. It's not what the kids want, it's not what your partner wants—it's what you NEED. By making this time for you, everyone will benefit. When we do what we really love to do, it's almost like taking a big, hot, soapy bubble bath —the impact on our physiology can be so revitalizing. In this section I am going to work with you to energize and repair your spirit.

CREATIVITY JOURNAL

To tap in to the spirit of who you are, begin to make a collage in your creativity journal. As you look at the pictures in magazines, ask yourself the question *What would engage my senses, and energize and heal me right now?* Let your intuition guide you to images of activities, places, and expressions on people's faces, bold words and soft colors and fabrics. . . . Once you begin to build the collage of your intuitive healing needs, let your imagination run wild and ask yourself how you can begin to gently introduce some of these ideas into your everyday life. Maybe you just need to buy a pink fluffy cushion, because it would feel great to have it around your face and body right now. Maybe you need to organize at least two nights in the week where you can head off to your bath to pamper your self back to life.

HEALING NATURE

I believe that nature is a natural and wonderful healer. The energy of plants and trees and the soothing sound of running water by the sea or a river all have a magical essence that can embrace our tired souls and spirits and begin to gently revitalize us back to life again.

I love to go out and walk on wet dewy grass when I get up in the morning—the sensation wakes me up on a deep level and invigorates every cell in my body. As adults, especially if we live in a city, we often forget about spending time in nature. I remember having a conversation with an on-site landscape gardener at a garden center who thought that garden centers are popular because people can connect with the energy of plants and trees. He believed that many people weren't aware of the healing impact of gardening, seeing it just as a hobby. For him the healing power of nature was at work as visitors to the garden center reconnected with nature, alleviating their stress and energizing their spirits in the process.

What do you like to do that brings you closer to the elements? Are your senses awake, and are you aware of the subtle energies around you? Go to your garden or to a park today and feel the energy of nature all around you.

VITAL INGREDIENTS FOR YOUR VERY OWN PAMPER PALACE

A clutter-free bathroom—make it clean, warm, and inviting.
No children's toys—put them in a bag/box that can easily be removed.
Some scented candles placed around the bathroom.
A soft neck pillow for your head when in the bath.
An extension cord and CD player to bring in relaxing music.
Some luxurious bubble baths.
Some essential oils that meet your needs.
A gorgeously scented body lotion.
A large fluffy white towel.
A novel or magazine.

HOW IT WORKS

The plan is that you book time at least twice a week to have a half hour of absolute relaxation.

You deserve this time so much.

If you warn your partner and your family that you are about to do this, they will then be prepared for the new habit to begin. The next thing to do is to set up your guidelines:
* Everyone must use the bathroom before you go in.
* Nobody should interrupt you.
*You don't take phone calls while you are there.
*You don't need to come out when someone needs something, except in an emergency!

This may sound harsh, but unless you set boundaries, everyone in your household will treat you as they always have, and as a result, you will be more stressed when you come out than when you went in!

The first and second times you do this, everyone is going to try their luck and interrupt you, but you must stay true to yourself and stick to your guidelines. By the third time you go in, they will get the message. This is the same as creating any new habit that will have an impact on others—they will continue to do what they have always done until they realize that they aren't getting what they want, then they will go somewhere else.

10 Steps to a New You—Relaxation

1. Each morning get up half an hour earlier than normal, if possible before anyone else wakes up. Appreciate the stillness of the house and the quiet of the day. Feel a sense of calm and anticipation about the day ahead. Make today special.

2. Light a candle and connect with the new day. If you have a garden, look out and appreciate the season and the weather for its positive qualities—if it's raining, it will feed the plants and trees; if it's gentle rain, feel it whisper on your palms; if it's windy, feel it blow the cobwebs away in your mind; if it's snowing, see it for its beauty and magic.

3. Begin the day by reading your affirmations and accelerators. Look in the mirror and repeat them over and over until you feel a connection in your heart and spirit. Really sense this new energy and feel the anticipation of the day ahead.

4. Play relaxing music or quiet music as you start your morning. Be aware that if you turn the radio or TV on, chances are you will be allowing in some bad news. Remember to limit yourself to one dose of bad news per day.

5. Establish what your goal will be for making this day special—it may be a walk in the park at lunchtime, it may be connecting with someone new, it may be creating a special meal for the family that night, or it may be reading your child

"Feel the energy of nature all around you."

a bedtime story while tucked up in bed with fresh clean sheets and a hot water bottle.

6. Sit down to a healthy dinner with your family. Try to make the meal one where everyone sits around the table and talks about the day. Switch off the TV and radio.

7. Make one special gesture to your partner and make them aware that you love them. Or connect with someone you love by writing a letter, sending an e-mail, or making a telephone call to a friend.

8. At least three times a week, take one hour to soak and reflect in your pamper palace.

9. Read your creativity journal to remind you of the adventures and feelings that lie ahead in your life. Feed your subconscious with the joy of how wonderful this life is going to be for you and allow it to go in search of the plans to bring your dreams to life.

10. Finally, get into bed at least half an hour earlier than normal, dim the lighting or light a candle, and write in your gratitude journal to remind you of all the reasons you can be thankful about your life.

AFFIRMATIONS

This planet is a magical mysterious adventure. I have the opportunity to explore it, if I choose.

*

I have the choices IN THIS MOMENT to DELVE IN and create a new reality.

*

TODAY I choose to Express LOVE in a creative way to the one I love. I honor my partner's support on this journey of life.

*

My relationships are wonderful. As I breathe life back into them, I watch them BLOSSOM AND GROW.

*

Today I choose to smile and positively connect with others. This makes me feel fantastic and opens doors.

The doors to my future happiness are open. I'm excited about what's around the corner.

*

I RELEASE ALL WORRIES about my future, I am connected to the magic of today. All is really well in my life.

*

I listen to my intuition. I KNOW WHAT IS BEST FOR ME. I have the courage to do what sets me free

*

Today I CHOOSE to do what I want to, not what I feel I should do . . .

*

I NOW focus on my HEALING journey by doing something I LOVE at least ONCE A DAY. I deserve this.

*

I Choose HARMONY and BALANCE in my life. This is a priority for my Health and Well-being.

*

I'm opening the DOORS to all the POSSIBILITIES in Life.

Dawn's Story ... As This Book Comes to an End

I'm sitting at the bottom of my garden, on a mossy old step with a pot of tea, breathing in the fresh, salty sea air and taking the time to appreciate the glorious, rugged Scottish scenery that lies before me on this crisp autumn day.

205

I moved here five years ago with a dream of teaching the principles of personal development to the world—but nobody knew who I was, and how could they take me seriously? I also had a dream of creating a beautiful home from a building site that was overrun with rats.

I came to this place full of dreams and aspirations. I had a clear vision of how I wanted my life to shape up. I had no money. I had no experience. I was terrified of speaking in public, but I had the greatest gift in the world . . . bags of determination and the will to succeed against all odds.

Today as I look at the house from the beach wall, I see a beautiful glass conservatory and a little cottage garden, which has all been created and shaped by the vision I had then.

I am so comfortable and alive in this place. I have had parties on the deck with my friends, and I have had many bonfires on the beach. I have so much fun here, I have laughed so much, and I've cried a lot, too!

However, like this book, everything comes to an end. My dreams that I shared with my friends five years ago are now being realized, and because of that I must step out of this magnificent comfort zone into the unknown where my ultimate dreams and aspirations lie.

Next week I move south to England, away from the sea, away from my family and from the rugged Scottish landscape to pursue my dream of taking this material out to the world through television and books.

Today I feel a slight sadness in my heart as I see my house being packed up. But I always know that I can come back here if things don't go as planned. That's the worst that can happen! Not that I think for a minute that will be the case.

My five years in this place have been a time of learning. I have learned to be totally independent and live on my own with my little girl. I have been on a deep emotional journey, and at times to unclog my soul, I needed the help of a professional to assist me in letting go of my past. I have faced so many fears, I have affirmed the best every day, and each morning I have lit a candle and given thanks for the wonders of the day I have just lived. I gave up running my company this year and learned to really trust someone else to do it for me; otherwise, I wouldn't have been able to free myself to do the things that my soul craves in my life.

There have been times when my life has felt unbearable—when we lost Mal, my magnificent stepfather, and when there were family challenges that we thought would never end. At times like this, sometimes we have to be patient and weather the storm.

On these days, the weight of life can feel too heavy to bear, and we just need to cry. I personally drink lots of creamy hot chocolate with marshmallows and chocolate sprinklings. I listen to music that makes me remember, I eat lots of goodies, and I drink good wine. Sometimes we just have to let go for a while, and for a time that is okay.

I find, however, that there comes a day or a night when the cloud begins to lift. As soon as I feel this, I go out to the cinema or rent a fun, light movie and begin to change my state of mind. I also begin to change the music I am listening to in the car or at home, until I hit on something that illuminates my soul.

I go out and buy lots of really healthy food and do some fun exercise to move my energy around, or I spend time in the garden. Then I'm ready to begin all the affirmations, gratitude journals, creativity journals, and daily personal-development reading again. After a week or so, I'm back on track.

I believe that life is a series of hurdles. I know that we all experience hardships and pain. That is the game of life, and nobody can avoid it.

The challenge we face is to learn how to bounce back and learn from the experiences we go through, and make sure that we don't make the same mistakes again. I really believe in being gentle with ourselves. We are only human, after all, and when we do something wrong, we can't undo it. We have to move on from our past or nothing ever changes. We need to treat ourselves as we would wish to be treated by someone who loves us deeply. When we learn to do so, we can find our wings and begin to fly!

The old cliché is true: As one door closes, another door opens—but only if you've got your chin up and your eyes wide open for all the opportunities that lie ahead of you in this magical world. The choice is yours; you have the ability to create your very own *Zest for Life,* and if this book doesn't help, get a professional to help you unclog your spirit. Your ideal life is out there, ripe for the picking. Only *you* have the key to the door to your fantastic future.

Good luck on your journey. Look into the eyes of yourself as a child, and be courageous. You deserve this chance. . . .

Love Dxxx

Dawn Breslin Workshops and Training Programs

ZEST FOR LIFE—DISCOVER YOUR TRUE POTENTIAL

This program has been designed to gently take you by the hand on a journey of self-discovery from childhood to present moment and beyond to a fabulous future. *Zest for Life* workshops present a great opportunity to revise dreams and ambitions, unlock your potential, and inspire you to live the life you're dreaming of!

- Change your mind-set from "simply existing" to "really living"
- Identify and overcome your limiting beliefs
- Renew your inspiration and conquer your fears
- Build up your confidence and rediscover your creativity
- Release your true potential
- Create a solid, focused, and personal vision
- Create a compelling and achievable life plan

FAST-TRACK YOUR POTENTIAL—MAXIMIZING HUMAN POTENTIAL

Our Fast-Track Your Potential program is an inspirational, intensive training session that has been described as a nine-hour personal coaching experience, taking attendees through an exciting program of self-discovery, motivation, focus, and change. This unique and personal course enables individuals to rediscover life balance and revise their working-life ambitions.

- Move beyond your restrictive limitations
- Increase your self-esteem and confidence
- Unlock your true potential
- Create a solid life plan
- Identify and overcome fears

TRAINING ACADEMY

If you are an experienced coach or trainer and would like to lead the current Dawn Breslin Workshops, The Dawn Breslin Training Academy offers you the opportunity to learn new skills in personal development and offer a range of ready-made programs to your client base.

We are looking for talented individuals who have:

- An incredible passion for personal development
- The ability to motivate, inspire, and develop individuals to achieve their dreams and ultimate aspirations
- Excellent communication skills

Every so often, right in the middle of an ordinary life, inspiration comes along and life becomes a fairy tale. . . .

If you would like to attend any of the Dawn Breslin Programs or would like further information, please contact the Dawn Breslin Team at: 011-31-468-7062 or *e-mail:* Info@dawnbreslin.com.

We hope you enjoyed this Hay House book.
If you would like to receive a free catalog
featuring additional Hay House books and products,
or if you would like information about the
Hay Foundation, please contact:

Hay House, Inc.
P.O. Box 5100
Carlsbad, CA 92018-5100
(760) 431-7695 or (800) 654-5126
(760) 431-6948 (fax) or (800) 650-5115 (fax)
www.hayhouse.com

***

Published and distributed in Australia by:
Hay House Australia, Ltd. • 18/36 Ralph St. • Alexandria NSW 2015
Phone: 612-9669-4299 • *Fax:* 612-9669-4144 • www.hayhouse.com.au

Published and distributed in the United Kingdom by:
Hay House UK, Ltd. • Unit 62, Canalot Studios • 222 Kensal Rd., London W10 5BN
Phone: 44-20-8962-1230 • *Fax:* 44-20-8962-1239 • www.hayhouse.co.uk

Published and distributed in the Republic of South Africa by:
Hay House SA (Pty), Ltd., P.O. Box 990, Witkoppen 2068
Phone/Fax: 2711-7012233 • orders@psdprom.co.za

Distributed in Canada by:
Raincoast • 9050 Shaughnessy St., Vancouver, B.C. V6P 6E5
Phone: (604) 323-7100 • *Fax:* (604) 323-2600

***

Sign up via the Hay House USA Website to receive the
Hay House online newsletter and stay informed about what's
going on with your favorite authors. You'll receive bimonthly announcements about:
Discounts and Offers, Special Events, Product Highlights, Free Excerpts, Giveaways, and more!
www.hayhouse.com